The
Tuned-In
Turned-On

Book About
Learning Problems

REVISED

Marnell L. Hayes

Academic Therapy Publications
Novato, California

Academic Therapy Publications
20 Commercial Boulevard
Novato, California 94949-6191

International Standard Book Number: 0-57128-090-1

3 2 1 0 9 8 7 6 5 4
0 9 8 7 6 5 4 3 2 1

Library of Congress Cataloging-in-Publication Data

Hayes, Marnell L.
    The tuned-in turned-on book about learning problems/Marnell L. Hayes;
{illustrator, Damon Rarey].
    p. cm.
    Includes bibliographical references.
    ISBN 1-57128-090-1
    1. Learning disabilities – United States. 2. Learning disabled children –
Education – United States. I. Title. II. Title: Tuned-in turned-on.
LB4705.H39   1994
371.91 – dc20
                                               94-3474
                                                 CIP

Contents

To Melanie and Colton

Preface to the Second Edition

It's hard to believe that it has been 20 years since I wrote this book. Since that time, the boys and girls for whom it was written have grown up, and many have children of their own. It has been fun to meet them and to hear how the book helped them so many years ago.

My daughter Valli, who helped me be sure that the book was helpful to students like her who had learning disabilities, is a grownup, too, and has two children! Her daughter, Melanie, does not have learning disabilities, and sometimes she is surprised at some of the problems that her mom and grandmother have. Little brother Colton is a toddler, and he will learn to appreciate his mother's strengths and weaknesses, too.

There are some changes in this new edition of *Tuned-In*, of course. There is a new chapter about ADD and ADHD, problems which didn't even have those names when the book was first written. I hope this chapter will help explain some of the many behaviors some students with learning disabilities may have.

I have also added a glossary at the back of the book. That's kind of like a dictionary, where you can look up words you don't know. I haven't put all the words in the book in the glossary, of course, because you already know most of them! I have tried to put in all the important words about learning disabilities, even though I have also tried to explain them as we come to them in the book. I hope this new section helps you. For example, if you want to, you can turn to the back of the book right now and look up the term *learning disability*. Don't you think this will be helpful as you go along?

I added the glossary because I put one in my book for grownups. (That book is called *You Don't Outgrow It: Living with Learning Disabilities,* and you may want to read it someday, too.) Then many of the people who used that book told me it was one of their favorite parts! Even when I was talking about some of the problems they had themselves, they didn't always know exactly how to define them. You will notice that I give examples sometimes, too.

There are also new chapters in the part for children to assign to their parents and teachers – that part was very short in the first edition! This time there's a whole chapter telling parents what their learning disabled child would like them to know and understand, and another chapter just for teachers.

Over the years, many teachers and parents have told me that *Tuned-In,* though it was written for children and teens, was the book that helped them the most because it was written so that anyone could understand it. I have tried to make the new parts easy to understand, too. I have also added new suggestions that I have learned since the book was first written. Most of the new ideas come from students I have talked to, who liked my ideas and wanted to share ideas of their own. I would love to hear from the new generation of readers, too.

"Dr. H."

Dr. Marnell L. Hayes
Department of Early Childhood and Special Education
Texas Woman's University
Denton, Texas 76204

It's More Than an Introduction

I'm glad to write this because I think anybody like me would like this book.

I used alot of the visual Handy-Dandy Hints. It helps me alot.

This book is good for any age person. I use the hints everyday. Mabey even 5 or 6 times a day.

My learning dissability is learning with my ears. I can't learn with my ears but I'm a good visual learner. I have to listen very carfully to what anybody says and use my eyes as much as possible so I can know and remember what they say.

But you'll have to understand if the author sounds like a mother sometimes its only because She *is* one. She's my mom.

Valli Hayes (age 12)
Junior Editorial Consultant

Introduction

This book is for kids (though I'd be pleased and proud if their parents and teachers read it, too). I've tried to write it so that it's interesting to read, and not *too* "preachy." My twelve-year-old daughter, one of the best visual learners I know (and, as she herself admits, one of the *poorest* auditory learners), has carefully edited my work, taking out as many "icky" parts as she could. I found her suggestions invariably useful, and her work contributed greatly to the manuscript.

Parts of the book have also been checked over by some other young people I know, including a young lady who's just beginning to read (so her mother reads the chapters to her), a boy who has just gone from a special learning disability class to a regular class, and a very bright young woman who had serious learning problems all through school, whose encouragement provided the final spurt of energy I needed to finish the book.

The ideas you'll find here came from many, many sources – some have become so much a part of me and my own learning processes that I can't remember *not* using them. Some came from teachers. But, not too strangely, most of the ideas came from kids.

Parents will want to read this book before, after, or with their children – preferably all three!

Anybody who reads this book will think of a dozen ideas I might have used, but didn't. That's good! When our ideas start multiplying, we're really on the right track. I'd love to hear some other crazy or strange learning and study ideas, especially ones from you kids. You can tell me how the book helped you, too.

"Dr. H."

Dr. Marnell L. Hayes
Department of Special Education
Texas Woman's University
Denton, TX 76204

Chapter One

"Who are you, and why are you writing this book?"

I'm a college professor, and I'm in the business of teaching teachers how to teach. That surprises many kids because it seems that teachers were just always teachers. Sometimes you don't realize that they had to *learn* to teach, and it was pretty hard for some of them! You should see me grade their papers. Sometimes I have to promise them not to tell their students what their grades are!

I also work with kids sometimes. I help to find out why they have trouble learning, or getting along with other people. I want to know what things are hard for them, and what things they do well, too. Then I try to help their teachers and parents decide what kinds of things will help them learn better.

Sometimes kids or parents want to know if they should stay in a regular class and get help from a tutor outside of school. Maybe they are thinking about a special class, or help from a resource teacher or a content mastery teacher at school. Or maybe they are thinking about a special school or program that might be better for their needs. Sometimes I can help them decide what would be best for their situation.

Sometimes, though, it is the student himself or herself who asks me for advice. Sometimes it seems that there is nobody who *can* help. Then I try to let the kids themselves know the best ways for them to learn.

I have had letters from young people, sometimes from other countries, describing their problems and asking for advice. I try to help them find someone closer to home who can help them. Sometimes we write back and forth for several years, like one girl in Canada who first wrote me when she was in a resource class, and years later when she was grownup in nursing school!

Kids teach *me*, too. One of the things that I have learned was that I have a learning disability. I always had trouble learning things that I heard. Oh, I was very good at learning from books, but understanding and remembering what I heard was very difficult. Foreign languages, which I would love to learn, are very hard for me because I have trouble learning and remembering the sounds that are different from English. I didn't understand why I had so much trouble until I began to see that many of my daughter's learning problems were the same ones I had myself.

One of the most important things that I have learned is that sometimes no one can help you as much as you can help yourself. After all, no matter how much your parents or your teachers care, nobody cares as much as you do yourself – because it's *your* life, right?

I remember one mother who came to talk to me about her son. He was 12 and going to start middle school the next year. He had been in a resource class for several years. He wanted to start middle school in regular class, with no special help for his learning disability. His mother was worried and wanted my advice.

What he had told her was that he just wanted to be a regular kid for one year. He promised her that if he failed, he would go to summer school to make up the work, or go back to resource class, or even a special school if she wanted him to. He said he would rather be a regular kid for one year, even if he failed. Of course, he also promised to try not to fail!

I thought she should let him try, and I told her so. If he failed everything, he might not finish high school as soon as planned, but he would know for sure that he needed help. He would also know how much he could do on his own.

The next year the mother called me. Her son was *not* failing – in fact, he was doing very well! She still had to help him with his homework sometimes, and he was thinking of taking a special reading class in the summer, but he was making it on his own!

I wrote this book for kids like him, and like you. I think kids want to know about their problems. I think that sometimes you worry a lot more when you *don't* know what's wrong, or what's going to happen, or what to do about it. I think you have a right to know, and to help your teachers and parents find the right ways to help you.

The problem is that sometimes adults think kids are too young to know about things. Problems at home, like money problems, or sickness, or family problems, seem to be problems for adults to deal with. Adults sometimes even think that *your* problems are their responsibility. And that is partly true, because they are responsible for you.

But you worry when you know something is wrong, and your parents or teachers won't talk to you about it. Sometimes you think the problems are much worse than they really are!

I had another very good reason for writing this book. My daughter was twelve years old, and she needed the information I put in the book. She needed to have it written down, not told to her, because that was the way she learned best. She helped me with the book by reading all the chapters as I wrote them. She often told me if the way I was saying things wasn't clear, or if I needed to explain things better. She also told me when the way I said things was too "icky," as she put it. Of course, I changed those parts right away! It was important to me that I said things in a way that kids (the little guys, the pre-teenagers like she was, and the teenagers) would be able – and willing – to use them.

Now, here's a question for you: Why are you reading this book?

Most likely, somebody gave you the book to read. Maybe it was your teacher, or one of your parents, or your doctor or counselor. Somebody thought that you were old enough, and – let's face it – *smart* enough to know what's going on.

You must be having some trouble in school. That *is* what this book is about, after all. Maybe reading is your problem. Or maybe it's math. Whatever it is, if I know kids, you have been trying to figure out why something that's easy for your friends is hard for you. It doesn't seem fair, does it?

Maybe you've already put a lot of thought into that. Maybe you think you've figured out what's wrong.

Maybe you've decided that you're dumb or stupid or maybe retarded, and nobody wants to hurt your feelings, so they're not telling you.

That's the first thing I can clear up for you.

You're not dumb or stupid. And you're not retarded. If you were, nobody would have told you to read this book. As a matter of fact, you wouldn't be able to understand the ideas in this book. Later, I'll explain more about how I know you're not dumb. But right now, let's get on with the business of finding out what is wrong.

The person who told you to read this book may have already told you what the problem is. If not, here it is: Your problem is what we call a learning disability, or LD for short. What that means is that basically, you're a pretty smart kid – at least average, and maybe even smarter – but that you have problems learning some kinds of things, or in some ways. You're not retarded; that would mean that you would have trouble learning everything. And you know that's not you!

There are some other words people use for learning disability, too. Some people like the word dyslexia. Instead of saying that you have a learning disability, they say you're dyslexic.

Some experts use the word dyslexia only for very serious reading problems, but now more and more people are using it to describe all kinds of learning disabilities. In this book, I'll be using the term learning disability most of the time, but if you'd rather say dyslexia, that's okay with me.

We'll also talk about some other kinds of problems people

14

with learning disabilities or dyslexia often have. One batch of problems is called ADD or ADHD. Some people who *don't* have LD or dyslexia have ADD or ADHD.

You may be interested to know that some pretty famous, extra smart people may have had learning disabilities. Did you know that Albert Einstein had a lot of trouble in school, especially in math? And the great Leonardo daVinci was a "mirror writer" – he wrote backward as well as he wrote forward! Even a man who was vice-president of the United States, Nelson Rockefeller, was learning disabled – he had very serious reading problems. And nobody, *but nobody*, could call these people dumb.

Some other famous people you may have heard of had learning disabilities, too. Cher, the singer and actress, has talked about her learning problems. So has actor Tom Cruise. They can be very proud of what they have accomplished in their lives – and so can you.

So having a learning disability is not at all the same as being retarded, because even part of the definition the experts use say you have to be as smart as average, or smarter!

This book was written to tell you more about what we mean by learning disability, and that's what the next chapter will do. Then there is a chapter that will give you some good ideas for studying, and some neat tricks to show your parents and teachers why some things are hard for you. There's a chapter about ADD, and how to work around some of your problems so that you can have more fun and get along with people.

The last part of the book has some reading that might be helpful for your teacher and your parents – chapters to let them know some of the things most kids with LD would like their parents and teachers to know. Why shouldn't you be able to assign some work to them for a change? After all, that's only fair!

Chapter Two

"What's a learning disability, or, if I'm so smart, why do I have trouble learning?"

One of the problems in talking about learning disabilities is that even the "experts" have trouble explaining it to each other!

Let's start with what you already know.

Some kids just don't have trouble learning anything. (Lucky!) They're good readers, good writers, good in math, spelling – everything. That's not you.

Some kids *do* have trouble learning – with everything from talking and walking to reading and math. Some kids have so much trouble learning that they may not even be in school, or may have to have special help even for dressing. That's pretty tough, but that's not you either.

Kids like you are really good at some things. And some things are just impossible. Let me tell you about some kids with learning disabilities that I've known.

1. Cathy was six, and in the first grade. She could read anything – even sixth grade books. But she had trouble sitting still and remembering anything her teacher told her.

2. Chuck was thirteen. He was a good reader, too, and pretty fair in math – but he couldn't write even one sentence. He could follow complicated repair books written for adults,

though, to take apart his motor bike and put it together again.

3. Beth was twenty. She was smarter than some of her teachers, but the counselor at her college thought she shouldn't even be there. Beth had a speech problem, but her learning problem was the biggest trouble. Whenever she tried to write, some of the words would "get lost" before she could get them on paper.

4. Billy was eleven, and a real "brain" in math. But he couldn't read a first-grade book.

5. Jeff was twelve. He was both a good baseball player, and good in reading and math. But he was always in trouble because he didn't even seem to notice when the teacher called on him. Sometimes he fooled around a lot in class, too.

Maybe one of these kids sounds a lot like you. Maybe not. The thing you probably noticed was that they all had some good points, and some bad ones. Just like you.

Maybe you can do anything on the computer – even figure out how to make it work when your dad has given up on it, but you can't seem to get your homework organized. Maybe you're the only one in the family who can program the VCR, but you can't manage to get to school with your gym clothes on the right day. The main thing is, you can do some things, maybe even better than most people, but there are some things you just can't seem to manage.

For a long time, the experts didn't even know there *was* such a thing as a learning disability. They knew there were kids like you who were plenty smart but who had trouble learning. They thought the problem was one of these things you've probably heard before:

"He doesn't try!"

"She could do it if she'd put her mind to it!"

"There's no discipline at home!"

"It's the parents' fault!"

"It's the school's fault!"

"It's the kid's fault!"

"If they'd cut out the TV and make him study, he could do it!"

"She just isn't motivated."

"If he'd behave himself, he could learn!"

Sound familiar?

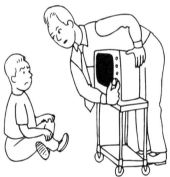

Finally the experts began to see that kids like you *did* try. (Sure, sometimes when you found out how tough it was, you gave up and pretended you didn't care – but that was after you *really* tried, and somebody wrote in red on your paper, "Why don't you try?" But you always cared, deep down.)

The experts began to see patterns in the way you learned and didn't learn. At last they came up with that name for the problems: Learning Disability.

The only problem then was that they explained it several different ways. Here are some of the things most of the experts seem to agree on.

First, they all seem to agree that you've got to be average or better in "smarts" to "qualify" for a learning disability!

Some experts noticed that kids like you do very poorly in some areas and very well in others (like my young friends I described to you earlier). We can show this on a chart, for an imaginary student named Bill:

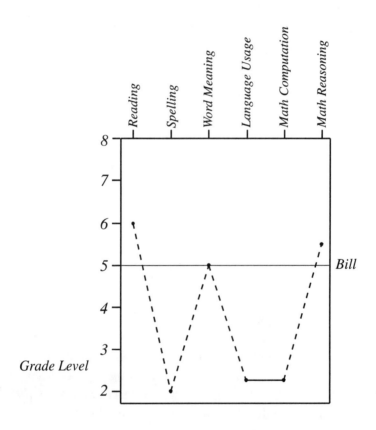

What this shows is that Bill is a fifth grader. He's a great reader – he reads like a sixth grader. But he doesn't spell any better than a second grader. He knows a lot of words, but his grammar is terrible. He's a sloppy math student, and makes a lot of errors; but he understands what he's supposed to be doing in those "story" problems.

All of this makes the dotted line on Bill's chart go up and down sharply, instead of along an even line at his grade level. We call it a "jagged profile." That's probably pretty much what your profile would look like, too, but maybe not in the same subjects.

A report card for Bill might show the same sort of thing – some good grades and some really terrible ones. The older Bill gets, the more likely all of those grades are to be low if somebody doesn't figure out what's wrong and help him. If you're in the sixth or seventh grade (or above) and you don't read very well, for example, you know you will run into trouble in social studies if the teacher wants you to do much reading.

Sometimes a learning disability is even more basic than a problem in reading or math. Often a learning disability can mean having problems with anything you have to learn by *seeing*. For some who may learn well with their eyes, it can be problems in learning what they *hear*.

This doesn't mean that the person needs glasses or a hearing aid. These students may have 20/20 vision or perfect hearing. It's just that what they try to learn with their eyes or with their ears gets mixed up, or too quickly forgotten.

What causes learning disabilities?

Don't we wish we knew! We are pretty sure that it has something to do with the ways in which our brains work, but we can't be sure just what.

For a while, most of the experts thought that learning disabilities were caused by damage or injury to the brain. That was because people (usually adults, like soldiers who had been hurt in battle) had learning problems and sometimes behavior problems that looked a lot like the learning problems and behavior problems that some children and teenagers had.

That idea made sense to a lot of people. Parents of a child with a learning problem would think back and remember a time when their child fell out of a high chair, or down the stairs, or off a tricycle. They thought that perhaps his or her brain had been damaged then.

The problem is, just about nobody can think of a child who *didn't* fall out of a high chair, or down the stairs, or off a tricycle!

The doctors would often do a type of medical test called an EEG, in which little wires are attached to the patient's head with a kind of jelly, and the brain waves are traced. (You may have had one of these tests – remember how hard it was to wash the goo out of your hair?)

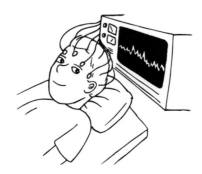

Very often, the EEG would be perfectly normal. And sometimes, when they checked people who learned very well, they found tracings that were *not* normal! So that didn't always give answers.

The experts finally decided that we couldn't really blame the problem on brain damage unless we knew there really was some damage – and the doctors couldn't very well open your head and take a look. Besides, "brain damage" sounds pretty scary and really doesn't tell what kind of trouble you're having.

Even though we don't know for sure what *does* cause learning disabilities, there are a lot of things we're pretty sure do *not* cause it.

I have already told you that having a learning disability does not mean being "dumb," or retarded. We also know that poor eyesight or bad hearing are not causes of learning disabilities. A learning disability is not caused by emotional problems – even though the kinds of problems you run into with a learning disability can cause you to feel pretty emotional sometimes, as I'm sure you know!

We have a pretty good idea that the problem *is* within the brain, though we don't know where, how, or why. What we *do* know is that your brain works pretty well in most ways, or you wouldn't be as smart as you are.

That gives you a pretty good idea of what a learning disability is, but let me sum it up.

A learning disability is a problem in one or more areas of learning. It can be in a specific school subject like math, reading, or language. It can be in a whole learning area, such as problems in learning things through seeing them or hearing them. While we may not know the cause, we know that it is *not* mental retardation, poor eyesight, bad hearing, or emotional problems.

Now let's find out how to learn more about your own special problems, OK?

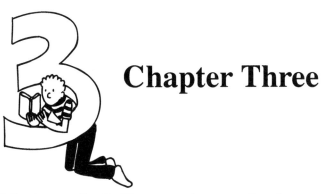

Chapter Three

"So how do I dig out the truth about myself?"

By now, you've figured out that if you're going to help yourself, you're going to need information. But where do you get this information?

If you are already getting some special help at school, then you already have at least one person who can help you find out what you need to know – the person who is giving you that special help. If you are in a special class, either all day or just for part of the day, then there is a great deal of information about you and how you learn.

Many years ago, not all boys and girls who needed special help for their learning disabilities were able to get that help. Finally, a law was passed that made certain rules for schools to follow to be sure that any student with a learning disability or other special problem could get the right kind of help.

The law was Public Law 94-142, the Education for All Handicapped Children Act. The law has been changed a few times since it was passed, but it has some very important parts that are the same.

The law said that in order for you to get that help, someone had to give you some special tests that would find out what things you were good at, and what things you could use help with. Then, a group of experts – your teacher, the person who gave you the tests, and maybe some others – had to meet with your parents to decide what kind of help would be best for you. They would have to meet again, at least once a year, to decide if the special assistance was helping, or if your program needed to be changed in some way.

An interesting part of the law said that if it was appropriate, you yourself could meet with that group of people so that you could let them know what you thought. Maybe you have been able to meet with your folks and the committee. If not, you might want to ask your parents if they think it might be a good idea for you.

So if you have been getting some help for your learning disability, there is information that you can find out. If you haven't had any special tests yet, you may be able to get that information afterward. We'll talk about those tests later on.

Here are some of the people who may be able to give you information that will help:

– Your teacher

– Your parents

– Your family doctor

– Your school counselor

It may turn out that none of them has *all* of the information you need, especially if you have not been getting special education help for your learning problem. Your teacher certainly knows how you are doing in class, and your parents will know a lot (maybe too much!) about your behavior. Your doctor, and probably your parents, too, will know how healthy you are. Your school counselor or your teacher may be the only one who knows how you did on any special tests you had at school (like achievement tests, where you work from special test booklets, and "bubble in" little circles on an answer sheet).

You may have to do some detective work to get the information you need. I will give you some of the questions you need to ask, and maybe that will help. You may know some of the answers to these questions yourself, without asking anyone else.

1. What do my teachers think is my biggest all-around

problem in school?

2. What's my very worst school subject?
3. What's my best school subject?
4. Have my eyes been checked lately? Were they OK? (If not, tell your parents that now is the time!)
5. Have I had a hearing test lately? How did it come out? (Again, if not, talk to your parents. They can probably get the school to give you a good hearing test.)
6. Have I had a check-up with the doctor lately? Am I pretty healthy, and am I getting enough sleep, and drinking plenty of milk, and all that other good stuff? (This is another must. To get the most from your body and brain, you've got to keep them in good working order. Computers don't work well if they're mistreated, and your body and brain are like a super computer!)
7. In what school subjects am I below grade level?
8. In what subjects am I doing grade-level work or better? If I'm not doing grade-level work in *any subject*, what seems to be preventing me (since I am average or smarter) from doing grade-level work or better?
   a. Is it my reading ability?
   b. Is it my spelling?
   c. Is it my writing?
   d. Could it be my listening skills?
   e. Is it my memory?
   f. How about my behavior? (Am I disorganized? Do I have trouble paying attention? Do I forget things? Am I distracted in class so I don't know what's going on? Am I not able to stick with one thing very long unless it's something I'm really interested in, like computer games or TV?)
   g. Or is it something else?

Once you have answers to these questions, you can begin to find out what to do about the problems you have uncovered. Ask your teacher to help you get the answers to these questions:

1. What did the tests show was my best way to learn – with my eyes or with my ears?

2. What is my weakest way of learning?

3. Should I do more eye learning, more ear learning, or more learning by doing?

If your teacher can tell you the answers to these questions, then you already are a step ahead! If you learn better with your eyes, you might be a *visual learner*. If so, you can go ahead to Chapter Five – Section 5-V, which will give you some special learning tricks that will make studying much easier for you. If you learn better with your ears, you might be an *auditory learner*. Move ahead to Chapter Five – Section 5-A, which is just for you.

Now, if you have already had a lot of special tests, you might want to read the rest of this chapter just to learn more about what they were for, and why they worked the way they did. If you haven't had special testing yet, then you will *definitely* want to read this part. It will help you understand why they're going to do some of the odd things they'll do.

First of all, you have certainly had *some* tests in school. You've had class tests, where you've traded papers with the person next to you to grade them. You've had tests that the teacher took up to grade and hand back to you.

You've also probably had some other tests called *achievement tests*. Those were probably in test booklets, and you had to use a pencil to "bubble in" the answers on a separate answer sheet. Those were not graded by your teacher, but were sent away to be graded by machines. A computer score sheet was sent back to your school and maybe your parents.

You may also have had some other tests that worked pretty much the same way, called *IQ tests*. Those were the ones that showed that no matter how well or badly you were doing in school, you were a pretty smart kid. "IQ" stands for *Intelligence Quotient*. If that sounds like a math term, it's because it is. It's the answer to a division problem that tells how smart you are compared to the average. It's just your mental age (the age level your brain thinks on) divided by your chronological age (how old you really were in years and months on the day you had the test). The exact score on IQ tests is usually not given to your parents or to you, but you may be told that you are "average," "close to average," or even "well above average."

For some kids with learning disabilities, taking the achievement tests and intelligence tests with a bunch of other kids is not a good idea. Sometimes the tests can't really show what they can do because they may be bothered by having so many noisy people around. Or they may have visual problems that give them trouble when they try to bubble in the answers. Or, if they have trouble reading, just reading the instructions can be a problem.

That's why special tests are given separately for kids who may have learning disabilities. These tests are a little different, and they are given with just one kid and just one special tester. And unless the test is a test of reading, you don't have to read any instructions! You also don't have to bubble in any answers, either.

You may take some of these special tests at your school, with the counselor, school psychologist, or diagnostician (those are all names for some of the people trained to do special tests). Or you may go to a clinic in a hospital, university, or special center. Wherever you have the tests, there are some things you will want to do.

First of all, you will want to be sure you get a good night's sleep the night before. You want to have your brain working at its best so that the tests will measure your best ability, so this is *not* a good night to stay up watching television! You will also want to have a good breakfast, and I *don't* mean a Twinkie and a Coke!

Wear comfortable clothes. You probably won't be doing anything very strenuous, but you don't want to be itchy or squirmy. If your testing is done at school, of course, you will be wearing regular school clothes.

If your testing is done at a special center or a clinic of some kind, you and your parents will have to sign in and perhaps fill out some paperwork. After a while, the person who will be doing your testing will meet you. Your parents won't be with you during the testing – it'll be just you and the tester.

The tester will introduce himself or herself, and will probably spend some time just getting to know you. This is a good time to ask any questions you might have about the testing. When I used to do lots of testing, I always enjoyed talking to the kids first. Sometimes I found that they were afraid I was a "shot doctor," or that some of the tests might hurt! They were always relieved to know nobody would let me give shots even if I wanted to! They were sometimes also surprised to find out that usually the tests were fun.

You may want to tell the tester that you have read this book, and let him or her know that someday you would like to know what some of your best areas are.

There is some information the tester will probably give you about the tests, but we'll go over it right now, anyway.

First of all, you may have more than one test. The tests will be chosen to help find out as much as possible about your particular problems in school. Some may just help to find out how you learn best. Others may be for information on how your brain or your eyes or ears work. Still others may test your ability in some school subjects.

There are some rules about testing that the tester will have to follow. One is that the tester will not be able to tell you if your answers are right or wrong! At first, this may bother you a little bit, especially if you are used to working with a special teacher who will let you know how close your answers are. The tester will only be allowed to let you know in general how you're doing, but not if any particular answer is right or wrong. And he or she will not be allowed to tell you the right answer if you don't know it, so don't ask. It's just one of the rules.

Another thing that bothers some kids is that each test may start out easy but it will get harder and harder, and you may feel as though you are missing lots of questions at the end. Don't let that upset you. The tests are supposed to start easy, and keep going until they are too hard. If you're ten, you may not miss any questions until you get to the eleven or twelve year level. Then you may start missing. You shouldn't feel bad *at all* to be missing things way above your age level! Of course, you won't know what level you're on, and the tester can't tell you. I always like to tell kids about this ahead of time, so they won't worry about it.

It will be important to try your best. If you aren't sure, give your best guess. Some tests may be timed, so you won't want to waste time, but you don't want to go so fast that you are careless. If you get tired or need to take a break, you will need to let the tester know in between tests, not right in the middle of a test. Most testers already plan to take a break sometimes, and may offer you a chance to go to the bathroom or get a drink.

It might be a good idea to mention that some testers might offer you a soft drink. Some experts think that soft drinks with sugar or soft drinks with caffeine, or even soft drinks with artificial sweetener, can affect how your brain works or your behavior. So it might be a good idea to stick to water only unless you and your parents have already discovered that you work best with or without soft drinks. After all, this information is important to you, so you want your best brainpower on display!

Some of the tests you might be asked to do are pretty interesting. You may answer some questions, put together some puzzles, remember a series of words or numbers, or copy some designs. You may read some, or work some math problems. You might be asked to describe a picture. Just give your best effort!

You will probably have some kinds of achievement tests, and you may have another IQ test. This one will probably give better results than the one you had at school with all the other students in the same room. Usually, when you have individual testing, you have a special IQ test that gives at least two different kinds of information – how well you do with verbal (word) information, and how well you do on performance (working with things). That's useful information to find out. Sometimes kids and grownups with learning disabilities are *much* better with one kind of information than another.

At some special clinics, you might also have some tests that involve walking on a beam (not a high one like gymnasts use!) or touching your nose with your eyes closed. And you could even have a brain wave test!

That one is called an EEG (electroencephalogram), and it's *very* interesting. You feel a lot like an astronaut, being prepared for space travel. A lot of tiny wires are attached to your head with little dabs of gooey glop, and you lie very still while the electrical energy in your brain (or something like that – honest!) traces little lines on a roll of paper. It's interpreted later by a specialist. Believe it or not, it's completely painless and can even be very restful. My daughter didn't like the glop in her hair, though, and could hardly wait to shampoo it out.

If you're being tested at a clinic, you might also be examined by a doctor. He or she might listen to your heart and lungs, of course, just like your family doctor does, but might also do some other things. I love the part where the doctor bonks my knees (gently!) with a little hammer to test my reflexes.

After all this testing, your parents will probably be pretty tired of waiting for you and reading the old magazines in the waiting room. At some clinics, you might have to go out to lunch and come back in the afternoon for more testing. If so, I vote for pizza! Often, though, just a morning or an afternoon will be enough.

You probably won't find out how you did on the tests right away. That's because the tests have to be checked carefully by the tester, and all the scores compared to what is expected. Then the tester will have to get together with any other people who have worked with you, and write a report. At some later time, your parents will have a chance to find out how you did. Depending on your age and maturity, you may get to come along for the conference. You will certainly want to ask your parents for information that the testers think will help you.

You might find out, for example, that you are a little smarter than average, but especially good at general information about the world around you and in vocabulary, and way below average in ability to see differences and copy designs. You may be at grade level in arithmetic computation (getting the answer when the problem is already set up for you) and not so good at arithmetic reasoning (working out story problems).

The tests may show that some of your problems are caused by visual problems – not the kind that mean you need glasses, but the kind that mean your eyes aren't working well together to get information or are causing it to get scrambled a little in your brain. Or it might be that some of your problems are because you have trouble telling the difference between similar sounds, so you misunderstand some things that you hear.

I think you can see how this information might help you and the experts figure out why someone as smart as you is having trouble in school. It can sometimes make it very easy to plan a program that will help you avoid your trouble areas and learn much faster and better. That's why it's important to do your very best on this testing. These tests don't get grades like A or B, but they can help you work out ways to get better grades in school. And that's where it counts!

Chapter Four

"What kind of learner am I?"

If you still don't have information you can use about the ways in which you learn best, this chapter may help you. It may be that your teacher wasn't able to help interpret all the tests you had in the past in a way that you could understand. Or maybe what you have tried has not been helping you.

What we're going to try to do in this chapter is find out some simple things about how you learn. What you will learn about yourself here is probably the same as some of the information in all those other tests, but we will look at it in an easier way.

Here are two lists. Look at them carefully, one item at a time. Someone can read them to you, and you can talk about each item with your teacher or parents if you like. Just be sure you put the answer *you* think is right for you.

There are no right or wrong answers here. You and your very best friend may have different answers every time, and both be right! You are going to be looking for some sentences that sound like they're talking about you.

Sometimes, the sentences may not exactly be describing a situation you have been in. Try to think of how you would feel in that situation and answer the questions the best you can. Remember, check the sentence if it sounds most like you. If it doesn't sound very much like you at all, leave it blank.

List A

_____1. People say you have *terrible* handwriting.

_____2. You don't like movies without sound, or games where you have to figure out what someone is acting out without words.

_____3. You'd rather do a music activity than art; and you'd rather listen to a tape than look at a display or pictures.

_____4. Your teacher says you leave out words, or sometimes you get words or letters backwards.

_____5. You can spell better out loud than when you have to write it down.

_____6. You remember things you talk about in class much better than stuff you have to read.

_____7. You don't copy from the chalkboard very well.

_____8. You like jokes or riddles better than crossword puzzles or comic strips.

_____9. You like games with a lot of action or noise better than quiet board games or puzzles you have to put together.

_____10. You understand better when you read aloud.

_____11. Sometimes you mess up in math because you don't notice whether it says to add or subtract, or because you read the numbers or directions wrong.

_____12. You're the last one to notice something new – that the classroom was painted, or that there's a new bulletin board display.

_____13. Map activities just are not your favorite – you never can seem to remember what continent Chile is in, or if Nebraska is north, east, south, or west of Missouri.

_____14. You often get in trouble for "sloppy work," even on workbook pages.

_____15. You use your finger as a "pointer" when you read, but you still get lost and skip words or lines sometimes.

_____16. Sometimes you get in trouble for humming or whistling to yourself when you're working.

_____17. Sometimes your eyes just "bother" you; but your eye tests come out okay, or you've already got glasses that the eye doctor says are just right for you.

_____18. You hate it when you get a bad, smudgy copy you are supposed to write on. It's hard to read.

_____19. "Matching" test questions, where you have to draw lines to the right answer, or you have to fill in the letters in order, or tests with those "bubble in" answer sheets, are a real problem.

_____20. Sometimes when you read, you mix up words that are almost alike – *pull* and *pill,* or *bale* and *dale.*

_____**Score**

List V

_____1. It seems like you're always having to ask somebody to repeat what he or she just said.

_____2. Sometimes you find yourself "tuned out" in class – staring out the window, maybe, when you were really trying to pay attention.

_____3. Often you know what you want to say, but you just can't think of the word. Sometimes you may even be accused of "talking with your hands," or calling something a "thingamajig" or "whatchacallit."

_____4. You may be going to speech therapy, or may have gone at some time in the past.

_____5. You have trouble understanding the teacher sometimes when you can't see his or her face.

_____6. It's usually easier to look and see what everybody else is doing than to ask the teacher to repeat the instructions.

_____7. When you watch TV or play music on your radio or CD player, someone is always yelling, "Turn that thing down!"

_____8. Your parents or teachers say you say "Huh?" too much.

_____9. You'd rather demonstrate how to do something than make an oral report where you have to talk in front of the class.

_____10. Words that sound almost alike (like _bill_ and _bell_ or _man_ and _men_) give you a lot of trouble. Sometimes you can't tell them apart.

_____11. You have trouble remembering your homework assignment unless your teacher writes it on the board or you write it down.

_____12. You like board games like checkers, or computer games like Tetris, better than listening games, or games where you have to copy a sound pattern, like Simon.

_____13. Sometimes you make mistakes in speaking (like saying "He got *expended* from school") that everybody but you thinks are funny.

_____14. You have to go over most of the alphabet in your mind or aloud to remember whether *M* comes before or after *R* and so forth.

_____15. You like doing art work better than music activities.

_____16. You do better when the teacher *shows* you what to do, not just *tells you*.

_____17. You can do lots of things that are hard to explain with words – like setting up a game on the computer, or doing interesting craft projects.

_____18. Your teacher is always telling you, "Answer in a complete sentence!" because you usually answer questions with just "yes," "no," or a single word.

_____19. Often you forget to give messages to people – when someone calls on the telephone for one of your parents, for example.

_____20. You're always drawing little pictures on the edges of your papers, or scribbling or "doodling" on scratch paper.

_____**Score**

Now let's look at your scores. Which is higher?

If List A is very much higher than List V, it gives us hints that your problems in learning are more with your *eyes,* and your best way of learning is with your *ears.* We might call you an *auditory learner.* You're going to learn some ways to use your ears and your voice to help you learn better than you could in any other way.

If your teacher or counselor agrees that the items you checked described you pretty well, then skip ahead to Chapter Five Section A. It will give you some study helps that work best for auditory learners like you.

If your List V score was much higher, then you tend to have problems learning with your *ears.* Your *eyes* will be your best keys to learning. You could be called a *visual learner.* You don't even have to read Section A of Chapter Five. Just skip right ahead to Section V. It's tailor-made for visual learners. It will help you learn to use your eyes to make learning easier.

And what happens if both scores are pretty close to the same? Well, if you have trouble in learning with your eyes *and* with your ears, then you'll need lots of help to get that average-or-better brain going! One problem you will find is that most learning after about third or fourth grade depends on using either your eyes or your ears.

You'll have to figure out ways to give those eyes and ears some help, with as much touching and doing as possible. You will need to experiment to see if combining touching and doing with looking or with hearing will help the most. Some of the ideas you will find in Chapter Six. Weird and Wonderful Ideas for Everybody, will be good for you. In it, you'll find some hints your parents and teachers won't believe!

Now, there's one more thing we can do to be sure we've got your problem figured out right. If you have already had a lot of special tests, either in school or at a special clinic, you may be able to get your teacher or your parents to find out if those tests gave information that agrees with what we have found in our checklists. If that information does *not* agree with the checklist, then go over the checklist again. If it *still* doesn't agree, then it might be a good idea to go along with the "experts." Try the section of the next chapter that goes along with what the tests found. If that doesn't help, well, then we'll go along with our very own opinions and our checklist!

Let's get going!

Chapter Five

"How can I make learning easier for myself?"

First of all, if you cheated and didn't read Chapter Four, you'd better go back! Only one part of this chapter is really for you, and Chapter Four tells you how to figure out which part it is.

Second, this chapter isn't going to "cure" your learning problem. Learning disability just isn't something you outgrow. I still have mine, but I have learned many ways to work around it and make it possible for me to do and learn the things I need to. You can learn to work around your learning disabilities, too.

Your classroom teacher, counselor, or maybe a resource teacher or special tutor are probably already working on remedial activities to improve the things you have the most trouble with in school. You and I can't dig out all the information they have since we aren't meeting face to face.

What we *will* do in this chapter, though, is help you make the most of the things you do *best*. This chapter will give you some ideas for studying that will help you learn the most as easily and quickly as possible.

We will try to give you some ideas that you will be able to use in particular school subjects, and also help you see how you might be able to think up ways to help yourself in many areas, at school and at home. Sometimes the best ideas are the ones you think up yourself.

So let's get started. Pick out the section for your own "learning style" and see what suggestions you can use.

Section 5-A
Super-Special Suggestions for Auditory Learners
(And for Auditory Learners only!
Visual Learners go to Section 5-V)

The first thing to remember is to tune in on voices! You will always do better when you *hear* the things you need to understand and remember. It doesn't matter whether it is spelling words or how to get to your friend's house – whatever goes in through your ears is what will most likely get to your brain, and stay there. You already know that you learn more from school lessons that were talked about in class. Why not use your *own* voice as a study aid, too?

It's even easier than it sounds. You just do all the studying you can, right out loud! Here's how you can use this idea in some different school subjects.

Reading

If you're having trouble in reading, ask if your beginning reading teacher used one of the "phonics" approaches. (*Phonics* means any one of several reading approaches in which students use the sounds of letters and groups of letters to figure out the words.) A phonics approach is probably the best one for you.

If you are already past the beginning reading stage, maybe you have stories or chapters that you have to read for school. You will understand them and remember them better if you read them out loud. If there isn't a quiet corner in the classroom where the teacher can let you read aloud to yourself, get permission to take the books home. You can sit in your room, or outside, and read aloud. Reading close into a corner may even help bounce the sound back into your ears better, and may help you keep your mind on your reading. Your ears will do the rest!

If you're really a pretty awful reader, see if you can get someone to read the material to you while you follow along. Or, if you're lucky enough to own (or borrow) a tape recorder, get someone to tape the material for you.

Many textbooks for older students can be borrowed from special services that provide taped books for blind students and students with serious reading problems. Sometimes it takes a while for new books to be available, but you can ask to have them taped as soon as possible.

A really good skill for you to work on is saying the words "inside your head" silently. If you practice this enough, it works almost as well as reading aloud. A good thing about this is that you can even do it in the library or anywhere else where you're not allowed to talk out loud!

I'm sure you've already noticed that when your teacher has you read silently in class, she said something like, "I said, *silently*!" or "I see some people moving their lips!" Well, the fact is, you were reading not-quite-silently because your brain "knew" you needed to hear the words to learn them best. The reason your teacher tried to get you to *stop* whispering the words or moving your lips is because she knows that people read more slowly that way. When you read aloud, you can't read faster than you can talk! But what your teacher maybe didn't know was that some people really *need* to say all the words. If you can't remember what you read, it is better to read slowly and *learn* than to speed along. Isn't that right?

Writing

Here's where that "talking to yourself" can come in handy again. If you often leave out letters or words, try it this way:

1. Plan the sentence you want to write by saying it out loud or silently.

2. Say it over two or three times until you're sure you've got it just the way you want it.
3. Then write it while you say it slowly.
4. Now read it aloud to check it.

If you're copying something, maybe from the board or from a book, try this:

1. Read the first few words or the first sentence.
2. Then close your eyes and repeat it to yourself until you've got it.
3. Then just write it out, saying it once more, slowly.
4. Now read it aloud to check it.

If you are in middle school or high school, and if you have to write a lot of papers, you can use a tape recorder as a special help. You can dictate each sentence as you plan it. Then you can play it back to make changes, and, finally, play it back one sentence at a time as you write it down.

If you have learned to type or work on the computer, you'll be much better at making up your own stories or term papers right at the typewriter than many visual learners are. Most of the computer programs for writing (called *word processing* programs) have spelling check programs built in, so you can go over your work to find any misspelled words. Also, if you find that you have left out a word, it's easy to go back and insert it. Many students with learning disabilities find that they are able to do very fine papers with the help of computers.

Spelling

We already know that you're probably not a very good speller. But even though you may not be able to spell the words exactly right, someone can usually tell exactly what word you are trying to spell, because you usually spell them just the way they sound. The trouble is, in English, the right spelling isn't always just the way the word sounds!

Studying spelling by writing the words five times each (which seems to be a pretty popular suggestion that most regular teachers make) is not a good way for you to study. Instead:

1. Say the word while you look at it. Then say each letter aloud. (Keep your finger on the word so you won't lose your place.) Say it this way: "Book, b-o-o-k, book."
2. Close your eyes and say and spell it again. Then open your eyes and check it.
3. Now close your eyes and say and spell it one more time.
4. Last, open your eyes and write the word, writing the letters by trying to hear them over again in your mind. Then check it. If you get it wrong, *mark it out* or erase it so you can't see it, and go through the steps again.

Now that you've studied the words, you can have someone call them out to you. Remember to "hear" the spelling of the word in your head before you start to write! This is the way to do it when you have a spelling test, too.

In the writing section above, we talked about the special spell check programs on some computers. There are also small spellers, which are electronic machines about the size of calculators, which are just for spelling. They are handy to have at school when you have material you have to write out by hand and you need help with spelling. There are several different kinds available, and they seem to be getting less expensive all the time.

Another spelling helper, which isn't battery operated, is the dictionary. If you are thinking that you never can look a word up in the dictionary because you can't spell it, relax! There are special dictionaries, made just for bad spellers, which list words by many of their most common misspellings, and then give the right spelling. This can be very useful to you as an auditory learner because you usually spell things just as they sound. These dictionaries are *terrible* for visual learners like me because when we see the wrong spelling in print, it makes an impression in our brains, and we tend to remember it that way!

There's one more important thing to say about spelling tests. Sometimes it is important to change the way a test is given so that a student with a learning disability can show what he or she has learned without the learning problem getting in the way. Some teachers may give a history test by asking the student to give the answers aloud rather than writing them down if the student is a very poor writer. (This is called a *modification*, and we even do it for some college students with learning disabilities, too.)

But taking a spelling test aloud is not a good idea! You probably spell better aloud than when you take a written spelling test, but think for just a minute: When does a person need to be able to spell a word? Why, when he or she is writing, of course! So the most sensible kind of spelling test is a written one.

Remember, *practice* aloud, but always end up by writing the word after you have practiced it.

Math

Those flash cards teachers like to use for math may not help you unless you find a way to turn them into signals your ears can use. Try it this way, starting with only three or four cards at a time:

1. First, look at the flash card on the answer side. (For example, let's say the problem is 3 x 2 = 6.) Read the whole thing aloud.
2. Then close your eyes and recite it several times.
3. Now, go on to the next two or three cards, doing the same thing. (Be sure you don't try to work on too many at one time.)

4. Then turn the cards over to the side without the answers. Read the first problem aloud and try to "hear" the answer in your head, and then say it.

5. Turn the card over, and check it. If you didn't get the right answer, fix it quickly by reading the *whole thing,* problem *and* answer, several times, and then saying it with your eyes closed.

If you need to learn your times tables or math formulas, using learning tapes with songs can help you. Even if the songs are silly and intended for younger kids, they can help you. After all, you can sing them over in your head; you don't have to sing them aloud where other people can hear you!

If there are things in math you have to learn that there are no tapes for, make up songs or cheers. You can use tunes you already know, and make the words as silly as you need to so that you can remember them.

Whenever you have trouble with math homework, try working the problem by explaining it to yourself out loud. Because of the way you learn best, you will often find your mistakes with your ears as soon as you hear them, even if your eyes have gone over the problem again and again. And, of course, it's always a good idea to read the instructions aloud to yourself before you even get started!

You will find some other math hints that you can use if you have trouble learning your times tables, in Chapter Six.

Foreign Languages

If you want to learn a foreign language, or if it is required in your school, you'll be way ahead as an auditory learner. That's because the best way to learn foreign language in general is with your ears, so you can pick up all the sounds that are different from English. (Lucky you – we visual learners have trouble with this!)

If you can get tapes of the particular book your school is using for the foreign language you are studying, that will probably help you the most. Play the tapes whenever you can. "Talk back" to the tape – repeat the words in the language, and just listen to the English part.

If you have vocabulary to study for a language test, make a tape. If you can get someone who has a very good accent in the language to make the tape for you, that's even better, but even your own voice is better than using written words. Listen to it as many times as you can, always saying the words back to the tape. First, put a learning section on the tape, which teaches you the words. Then have a study section, which helps you test yourself and study. You might try it this way, for a vocabulary lesson in Hebrew:

"Here are the vocabulary words for this lesson. Repeat the words after the speaker.

The word for *tree* is *etz.* (pause)
The word for *flower* is *perach.* (pause)
The word for *branch* is *anaf.*" (pause)

(and so on, through the list you have to learn.)

"Now listen to the word in English, and then say the word in Hebrew. If you get it right, repeat it again after the tape. If you don't know it or you get it wrong, repeat it *several times.* Here are the words:

tree (pause)   *etz* (pause)
flower (pause)   *perach* (pause)
branch (pause)   *anaf"* (pause)

Your main problem in foreign language is likely to be spelling. If so, you may want to put the spelling of the words on the tape, too.

Your teacher may suggest you learn from flash cards, and your language book may even have a set of flash cards that come with it. Flash cards just aren't right for you. You can use the flash cards, though, as a guide to help you make your tape, to be sure you've put all the words you need to learn on the tape.

Other School Subjects

Talk, talk, talk! *Listen* to yourself talk about all your school subjects. If you have to study a map, go over it and tell yourself all about it, sort of like this:

"Well, I see Florida down there, looking kinda like a thumb. That great big one over there is Texas. And up here, separate from the others, is Alaska . . . " and so on.

You can do this with other subjects, too. If you're a good reader, just read it out loud and listen to yourself. You can read from the book, or from notes, or from a study outline. If you're *not* a good reader, you can get someone to read to you, or a parent or friend or maybe a peer tutor to help you study by talking with you about the subject. It doesn't matter whether it's history, science, or health – just "talk it up."

If you have notes to study for a test, or if someone has highlighted a chapter for you to study (maybe using one of those colored markers, which are really better for visual learners), don't waste time looking at these materials over and over. Read them aloud! Reading the important parts or outlines just one or two times can be more powerful for you than looking at them for hours. Remember, use your ears!

Special Study Tips

Another way to use your voice and your ears to help you study is to make up raps or cheers to help you learn things. It may sound silly, but it can be fun – and it works. Try this one, for example:

Gonna learn the parts of flowers,
Before I get to school,
Gonna learn 'em now,
Don't wanna be a fool!
Petals are the colored parts,
Sepals are small and green,

Bees buzz around them.
Lookin' kinda mean.
Stamens hold the pollen,
Pistil takes it in,
Now I know those 4 parts,
And I can say, "Amen!"

I'm sure you can make up a *much* better rap than I can. How about one to learn the state capitals, or the major rivers of your state? Any time you have a *list* of things you need to learn, there's the chance that one or two of them will drop out of your memory when it's time to take a test. With a memory aid of any kind, it's easier for you to pull names or lists back from your memory so that you don't leave any out.

You probably learned the alphabet with the aid of the "Alphabet Song" or used the "Thirty Days Hath September" song to help you figure out whether May has 30 or 31 days. There are many such useful poems and songs for helping people remember important facts.

Some people think the memory devices are harder to remember than the original facts. That's fine for them – maybe they don't have learning disabilities, or maybe they just haven't discovered how much fun such memory aids can be.

It's okay to let your memory ideas get pretty complicated if it helps you remember. I love history, but I'm not very good at remembering some of the facts in order. I really like the poem for remembering what happened to the wives of King Henry the Eighth:

King Henry the Eighth to six wives was wedded,
One died, one survived, two divorced, two beheaded.

It's grisly, but it worked for me. Then a few years ago, I was excited when I found two more poems to help me remember some facts about them. The first one tells the order in which he married them:

Kate, Anne, Jane;
Then Anne, and two Kates again.

(You have to pronounce *again* the English way, to make it rhyme with *Jane,* not the American way, which rhymes with *begin.*)

The second poem tells what happened to each one in order:
Divorced, beheaded, died,
Divorced, beheaded, survived.

Since Henry the Eighth managed to marry three different women named Kate, and two named Anne, my only problem now is to straighten out their last names so I know *which* Kate and *which* Anne! Maybe I can remember "*A B*ad *S*cene, *CH*o*P*ping off heads!" That gives me *A*ragon, *B*oleyn, *S*eymour, *C*leves, *H*oward, *P*arr. There! I think I've finally got it right at last! (Note: If you're listening to this book on tape, that part was probably confusing, even if you *are* an auditory learner. You will want to play that part again a couple of times, or look at the book so that you can see how the letters are the same.)

You may find that a tape recorder is a lot of help to you. Instead of writing out notes or an outline, try putting it on tape. You can tape record your own study raps or memory tricks, and play them back to yourself, reciting along with the tape to help get things into your memory.

You can also benefit from books on tape. As a person with a learning disability, you are entitled to use the services that used to be available only to people who are blind. Now these services are available to people who are "print impaired," or who have learning disabilities such as dyslexia. If you need taped material to help you learn, you may qualify. Ask your parents to check on the resources listed in the parents' section in the back of this book.

You can probably think up many more ideas to use your own voice and your ears to help you learn. It doesn't have to be hard, serious work all the time – the more fun it is for you, the easier it will be for you to remember. And by the way, if some of your friends think some of these study helps are weird, just you wait. Pretty soon they'll be using your ideas, too!

Now skip ahead to Chapter Six for some crazy ideas you won't believe until you've tried them! (Remember, don't read the next section. It's for visual learners, and they don't learn the way you do at all. They're not allowed to read your section, either!)

Section 5-V
Handy-Dandy Hints for Visual Learners
(And for Visual Learners only*!*
Auditory Learners should go back and read Section 5-A.
If you've already read that section, then skip to the next chapter.)

Look and learn – that's your byword. You'll need to use your eyes for your best learning. You already know that what you've seen, you're more likely to remember. When you see a movie, you're the one who remembers all the details – maybe sometimes even better than your teacher or your parents!

Your secret weapon will be learning how to make "mind pictures" out of things you see and hear. And it's easier than it sounds. You already know how to do it; you just have to do it more. For example, if somebody says "butterfly," many of your classmates just hear the word. But you *see* a butterfly in "living color" in your mind's eye! You may even be surprised that some people *can't* do this. They can't even imagine how their bedroom would look with a shaggy red bedspread and blue pennants on the wall, or whether a silver glitter helmet will look awesome or just awful with a green 'cycle.

You can use your ability to "see" and imagine. Whether it's just remembering three things you have to take to school tomorrow or how to spell a word, making pictures in your mind can help you. If you're on your way to get those three things for school, try to see them in your mind – the backpack, the gym clothes, the money for the field trip – and then you are less likely to forget them. Ask someone to write that new word for you, or to spell it so you can either *really* write it, or try to see the letters lining themselves up in your mind. "See" how easy it is?

What's more, you can just turn the spoken words your teacher uses into pictures, too! Let's see how this works with different school subjects.

Reading

The kind of reading approach that's best for you would be a "look-and-say" (sometimes called "see and say") approach to begin with. (That's an approach that uses lots of pictures, and words that you learn by memory just from seeing them many times along with the pictures and in short sentences.)

If you're still a beginning reader, you or your parents may want to talk to your teacher and find out what kind of method he or she is using. If it's a "phonics" method, woe is you! In a phonics approach, you learn the sounds of individual letters and groups of letters, and learn to put the sounds together into words. That's hard for visual learners like you.

Perhaps your parents or school counselor can talk to your teacher about the best method for you. There are many good methods for teaching beginning reading which use the *eyes* more than the ears – and that's for you.

Sight words, flash cards, and experience stories will be things your teacher will use. If you're already reading, but are getting help to be a better reader, you will do better if you *don't* try to "sound out" new words. Instead, look at the word. Does it *look* like some of the "sight" words that you already know? After you've figured out what word it looks like, then you can try to figure out what letters (and sounds) are different. This means that looking at the whole word comes first. Then you may only have to sound out one or two letters, not all of them!

If you have begun to read using a "look-and-say" approach, after you have a good supply of words in your memory, you can begin to learn some of the phonics information that you will need to help you figure out new, unfamiliar words. A good way to do that is to study "word families," or words that are alike except for one letter.

For example, *ball, tall, fall,* and *call* just have a different beginning letter, and they rhyme. After visual learners like you get used to just one letter that is different, their eyes can help their ears learn to figure out new words. Flash cards, with sets of words with only the first, last or middle letter that is different, can help. Try *man-can-fan,* or *bill-bell-ball,* or *ban-bar-bat* – you can make many more than these.

Writing

You may need to go over anything you write more than once. You'll probably leave out a word or two, or do some weird spelling, because most people make up things they want to write by "hearing" them in their minds first and then writing them down. That's hard for you, just as it's hard for you to write down what the teacher says unless she or he writes it on the board. Getting things into your head through your ears just isn't your best thing!

One way to catch your mistakes in writing before the teacher does is to write what authors call a "rough draft." This is a messy copy that you will correct and rewrite. For example, when you write a book report for the first time, skip lines. That way you have plenty of room to fit in whatever you might leave out, or might want to add later.

After you've written your rough draft and checked it for errors or better ways to say things, then recopy it. You'll make fewer errors if you use a sheet of paper or ruler as a guide under each line of your rough draft as you copy it. That way you won't get lost and end up copying the wrong line by mistake.

Writing a rough draft first *does* take more time. That means you have to be a good planner, so you won't run out of time! This isn't so important for homework, term papers, or book reports. But when you only have a certain amount of time, like during a test, you can't waste *any* time when you know you're going to have to copy your paper over.

A good way to be sure you write everything you want to say without wasting too much time is to make a very quick outline, right on the margin of your paper. It doesn't have to be fancy – just enough to remind you of the points you want to make, like this:

General Custer

1. His record
2. His temper and vanity
3. Little Big Horn
   a. Custer's mistakes
   b. Number killed
   c. What happened later

What happens if you run out of time, and you haven't finished recopying your answer? First, ask the teacher to give you more time. If that's not possible, then turn in what you have – rough draft and outline, too. Your teacher can see that you had a good answer, and may give credit, even if he or she has to wade through your rough draft to find it!

Copying from the board or a book is easy for you if you do it this way:

1. Look at the whole word or sentence.
2. Close your eyes and try to "see" the picture of it in your mind, just as it is written.
3. Then, instead of looking back and forth from the board to your paper, you just copy it from the picture in your mind.

With practice, you can get good at this. You'll learn just how many words at a time (or maybe even how many sentences!) you can remember. And this is something only visual learners like you *can* do well.

Working on the computer is great fun for writing, too. You can type in your rough draft and then go back and change mistakes, add things you think of later, and improve it. Then you can print a copy and look at it again for improvements you want to make before you make your final copy. Some computers have spell check programs, so that you can find any nasty spelling errors before you turn your paper in.

As a visual learner, you might like using the kinds of computer programs that use *icons*, little pictures, to tell you what steps to take next. (Auditory learners sometimes have trouble remembering what all the icons stand for. You may have to help them out!) There's more about computers in Chapter Six, Weird and Wonderful Ideas for Everybody.

Spelling

You've got to "see" the words to spell them. Study new words with your eyes this way. Look at the word first; then close your eyes and make a picture of the word in your mind. Then just read the letters from the "picture!" Using this method, many visual learners become excellent spellers!

Another way to work on spelling – *after* you've done plenty of that "picture making" – is to write each new word a few times. Look at the word, see it in your mind's eye, and write it. Check it and then copy it once or twice.

If someone wants to call the words out to you to help you study your spelling, that's not a good idea for you. But if you want to study for a spelling bee in which you *have* to spell the words out loud, do it this way: When the word is read, close your eyes and try to picture it. Then just read the letters off the picture. It works! You can even keep your eyes closed if it helps you concentrate better.

Math

Flash cards were practically invented for you! Use them to study math combinations or, if you're a high school student, to study formulas.

Let's use easy math combinations as an example of how visual learners should use flash cards.

First, your flash card should have two sides – one with the problem, and one with *both* the problem and the answer (not just the answer!) Look at the problem side. If you know the answer, say it and try to "see" it in the blank. Then turn the card over and look at the answer. If you were wrong, run your eyes over the problem and correct answer *several* times, so that you can get the correction "photographed" in your mind. This is very important for you as a visual learner. You don't want to leave the picture you made in your mind of the *wrong* answer!

The next step is to put the card back in the stack you are studying, just a few cards down. You want it to come back up again soon, so that you can get it right!

When you have *new* math combinations or formulas you need to learn, start with the side with the answer! Look at the problem and answer a few times. Then turn the card over and try to "see" the answer in the blank. Turn back to the answer side and check.

If you have trouble working "story" problems in math, try to visualize (see in your mind) all the items or people in the problem. For example, if it says, "Three boys each have three apples . . . " imagine those boys and those apples. It'll help! If you need stronger pictures, just draw little sketches on a sheet of scratch paper while you're working the problems.

Foreign Language

Foreign language is a special problem for visual learners. Because so much of learning a new language depends on being able to hear and understand all new words and sometimes even new sounds, it's hard for people who learn better with their eyes.

You may be required to learn a foreign language in your school, or it may be something you just really want to do. If so, there are some hints that can make it a little easier.

First of all, if your school uses a "conversational" approach (one in which you learn mainly by speaking with the teacher rather than using a book or workbook), or an audio-lab approach (one in which there is a lot of work with taped material), you will need to have some modifications.

For visual learners, it's important to have written material to look at, especially while listening to tapes or doing word drills. It is difficult for you to hear and understand those different sound combinations; seeing them written helps you learn to understand more easily, especially in the beginning.

Of course, you can't use printed text for conversational language learning. But you *can* ask the teacher to provide you a written list of the new words she or he expects to be including in the next lesson, or a written table of the verbs that will be used.

You will want to make flash cards to study, study, study the vocabulary. Put the foreign word on one side of the card, and the English word on the other.

Begin with just a few cards. Go through the foreign side first and see if you can remember what any of them mean in English. If you don't remember one, turn it over and look at the English. Then turn back and forth several times until you get the word in both languages strongly in your mind. Then go through the whole stack again, still with the foreign side up. Do this until you have mastered all of them.

Now, the more difficult part. This time go through the stack with the English side up. It will be harder to pull the foreign word out of your memory. When you get one wrong, or can't think of it, repeat the step of looking back and forth from one side to the other until you get it. Then put the card back in the stack, just a few cards away, so that it will come up again soon.

A friendly word of warning: As a visual learner, you may have trouble ever developing a very good accent in a foreign language. You'll probably always be noticed right away as someone who's not a native speaker!

Some students with learning disabilities have a great deal of trouble learning foreign languages. Since some colleges require a foreign language, teenagers with learning disabilities who have serious problems with a foreign language who are planning to go to college need to be sure the college they are considering either does not have this requirement or is willing to make a modification to permit the student to take some other subject instead.

Other School Subjects

Look at everything. Use your eyes constantly. Look at pictures, maps, and charts. If you can learn to make very short outlines for things you have to study, you can look them over just before tests. As a matter of fact, just looking carefully at your notes or an outline of the material may help you more than spending lots of time studying things aloud with a friend or peer tutor.

Acronyms are good study helps, too. An acronym is a word made up of the first letters of a list of things you need to study. It's easier to say UNICEF than United Nations International Children's Emergency Fund, right? If you need to remember a list of things, make up a silly acronym. It doesn't even have to form a real word, if it is easy to remember. Some people use the made-up name *Roy G. Biv* to remember the colors of the rainbow: *R*ed,

*O*range, *Y*ellow, *G*reen, *B*lue, *I*ndigo, and *V*iolet.

And speaking of colors, you can use them to help you learn, too. Visual learners often find that making colored notes, or even underlining or highlighting in color, can help boost those mental pictures. Auditory learners can use tape recorders, which are expensive.

You can do better (and cheaper) as a visual learner by stocking up on all sorts of paper – some white, some lined, some colored; some in a variety of notebooks; lots of fine-point felt-tip pens in colors and fluorescent highlighter markers; and colored sticky-notes (they come in more colors than just yellow, which most people use). You'll want colored index cards to use for flash cards, and some of those zipper-type small plastic bags to organize them in. And maybe you'd better also get a backpack to carry all this junk in!

A note about highlighting – many schools recommend it for students with learning disabilities. You will want to experiment to find out if it works for you. Some visual learners (and I am one of them) are distracted by highlighting and can't use it. I mark along the *edge* – out in the margin – of a part I need to remember. With a little trying out, you can find the best method for you.

Sometimes highlighting is not allowed because students have to turn the books in at the end of the year without marks in them. If that's so at your school, find out if your parents can buy a set of books for you that you *can* mark in.

Another problem with highlighting is that some schools have teacher's aides who highlight the books ahead of time for students with learning disabilities. This is not a good idea! The person who will use the book should do the highlighting. Sometimes just using that marker will help your eyes take in and remember the material. The teacher or the aide can sit next to you and show you the important parts to mark, but you need to do it yourself.

In all your studying, be sure to give yourself all the visual help you can. Make lists! Write notes to yourself! Write down all your homework assignments – that's better than not remembering what you had to do. Also, get your parents in the note-writing habit, too. The best place for their reminders to you (or your messages to them) may be right on the refrigerator door. That's one place none of us snacksters seem to miss!

It's a good idea to keep a little note pad with you all the time at school. Then you're set to make notes before you forget – whether it's about your homework or a reminder for your parents about something.

Be sure to keep a pencil and notepad next to every telephone in the house, too. If you take messages over the telephone, you are likely to forget – not just what the message was, but even that somebody called at all! Remember, over the telephone there are no pictures, so there's nothing for your good visual memory to work on! (At least, there are not any TV phones *yet*. They are sure to be in every home before too long!)

In your room at home, you will want to have a bulletin board of some kind to put up things you need to remember. Another useful kind of board would be either an old-fashioned chalkboard, or, even better, a whiteboard (the kind that uses dry-erase colored markers). That way you can keep your messages to yourself up-to-date and color coded!

If you're in the middle school or high school and you have understanding teachers, you can ask them to look over the notes you take in class. You may miss some of the things you heard, but if they help you get them in your notes so your eyes can work on them, you've got it made! If you have a *lot* of trouble taking notes, ask for a note-taker – one of the other students who is a good note-taker can give you a copy of his or her notes. This can be written in your educational plan if you are getting special education services at your school.

Remember, your eyes can do your learning for you, but only if you provide the right things for them to see.

Now look ahead to Chapter Six for some strange study ideas. Some may be just right for you!

Chapter Six

Weird and Wonderful Ideas for Everybody

Not all of these hints will be just right for you. Some will be
solutions to problems you don't even have! Try out some of the
crazy study hints, though; and at least take a good look at (or
listen to!) some of the other ideas. There just may be a suggestion
you can use, or maybe an inspiration for an idea you think up
yourself that will help you!

Multiplying on Your Fingers

Here's one *nobody* believes – at least, not until they've tried it.
It's a counting-on-your-fingers method for doing multiplication.

First of all, chances are you've been counting on your fingers
for math all along – but you may have had to do it under your
desk because your teacher didn't approve. I'd better explain that I
do approve of counting on your fingers – I couldn't add or
subtract if I didn't!

Now, here's how this method works. (You'll have to put this
book down and really *do* it to learn it.) This works for any
multiplication combination from 6 to 10. (You won't need the
10's, though. They're easy!) You'll have to learn up through the 5's
the "old" way – by memorizing them.

Make fists and stick up both thumbs. You'll just have to remember that *thumbs are 6's* – to help you remember, we'll call this the "Thumbs are 6's" method.

Now we'll do 7 x 8. We count up each number we want to multiply, one on each hand, starting on either hand (you don't have to remember left and right!) by sticking out fingers, always starting with the thumb, which is 6:

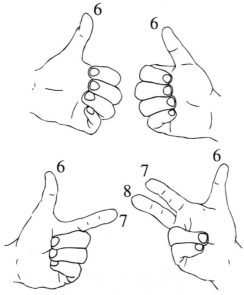

Now, some of your fingers are sticking out and some are curled in. Count the sticking-out ones by 10's (10-20-30-40-50), and you get 50. Think 50 very strongly in your mind – say it aloud if you need to.

Now look at the curled-up fingers. You have two on one hand, and three on the other. Multiply these small numbers in your head (2 x 3 = 6) and you get 6. Now add the 50 from your mind (50 + 6 = 56) and you get 56.

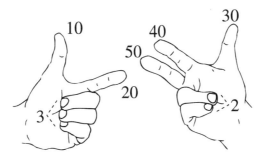

Neat trick, huh?

You may be thinking that's a pretty complicated thing to learn. It is – but if you have trouble memorizing the times tables, every time you "guess" wrong, you've been putting error messages into your brain, making it harder and harder to memorize them. With this method, you *will* get the right answer.

I teach this method to teachers, so that they can help their students. And sometimes they have a hard time learning it at first, but they tell me their students catch on right away. If you're an auditory learner, you'll want to do your counting out loud, almost chanting. Look at this example, with 7 x 7:

"7 times 7. (on one hand) 6-7. (on the other hand) 6-7. Now, 10-20-30-40. Remember 40! Curled up, (on one hand) 3, (on the other hand) 3; 3x3 makes 9; 49!"

After a while, you'll find that you'll *start* to stick out your fingers to get a multiplication fact, and the right answer will pop into your head before you're even finished. That's good! That means you're beginning to memorize them. Don't worry if you're not sure every time – you can always remember "Thumbs are 6's" to check it out.

If you're still not sure you've got it, try a couple more combinations. To do some, you need pretty flexible fingers! When you're sure you understand, go teach it to someone else – that's the best way to be sure you've really got it. Teach it to your teacher for a special treat. Maybe if you do, she or he will understand that counting on fingers is okay after all!

Getting Numbers Straight

Some students with learning disabilities have problems writing their numerals the right way around – sometimes they come out backwards. If you have that problem, here's a method for you.

First, you have to learn this a different way if you're left-handed than if you're right-handed. So let's do lefties first.

For Lefties Only – Righties Go Ahead to the Next Section!

You probably don't have trouble knowing which way to write all of the numerals, but here are the instructions for all of them anyway. Pick the ones you have trouble with.

First, not all the numerals are a problem. Take the 1, for example. It can't be backwards, really. So we won't worry about it. You can make an 8 in a way many teachers would call wrong, but it still looks fine, so we won't worry about it either. All the others can be a problem, so here's how we check them.

This method is called "Sixes Don't Fit" because it works for everything except 6.* We just have to remember that 6 goes the other way.

Write down the rest of the numbers, nice and big and then *keep the pencil in your hand.* Now take the hand that isn't busy holding the pencil, and look at it. It curves this way:

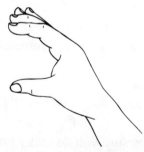

* Adapted from Connor, Madge M. 1980. Hand checking and six doesn't mix: Remediation of digit reversals. *Academic Therapy, 16,* pp. 207-210.

Look at the numeral 2. If the big, open curved part curves the same way as your hand, it's correct.

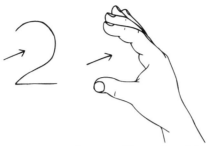

The 3 has two open curved parts. They should curve the same way as your hand, too.

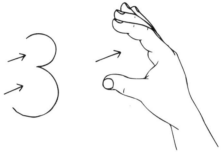

The 4 can be made two ways, either with a point at the top or an open part at the top. If you make it with an open top, that part points up, and we won't worry about it. Hold your non-pencil hand flat, and point your thumb down. The *bottom* open part of the 4 should match the opening between your thumb and your fingers.

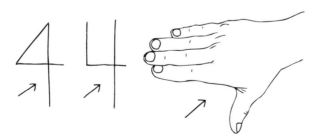

A 5 has a round open part, and a squarish one. Look at the round open part. It should be the same as your non-pencil hand.

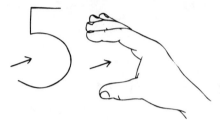

Whoops! Remember, "Sixes Don't Fit," so the 6 should be the other way. (If you can't be sure it's the other way, check it with your *other* hand).

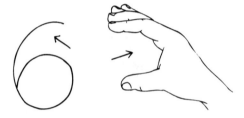

A 7 is just one big open part. Put your hand flat, with the thumb down. The open part between your thumb and fingers should match the 7.

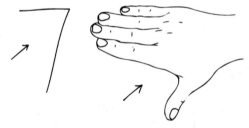

The 9 has a funny shaped open part, but it should match your non-pencil hand, too.

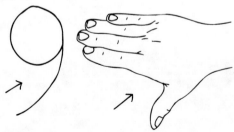

At first, you may want to use this method just when you've written a numeral and you're not sure if it's right or not. Later, maybe you will want to use it *before* you write. Pretty soon, you'll have practiced doing it right so many times that you probably won't need to check any more at all!

For Righties Only – Lefties Should Go Back to the Part Before

You probably don't have trouble knowing which way to write all of the numerals, but here are the instructions for all of them, anyway. Pick the ones you have trouble with.

First, not all the numerals are a problem. Take the 1, for example. It can't be backwards, really. So we won't worry about it. You can make an 8 in a way many teachers would call wrong, but it still looks fine, so we won't worry about it either. All the others can be a problem, so here's how we check them.

This method is called "Sixes Don't Fit," because it works for everything except 6. We just have to remember that 6 goes the other way.

Write down the rest of the numbers, nice and big, and then *put the pencil down.* Now look at your pencil hand. It curves this way:

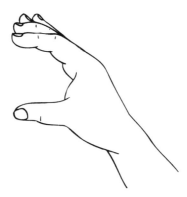

Look at the numeral 2. If the big, open curved part curves the same way as your pencil hand, it's correct.

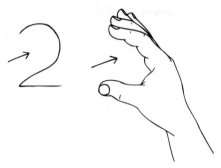

The 3 has two open curved parts. They should curve the same way as your pencil hand, too.

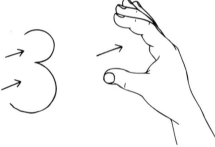

The 4 can be made two ways, either with a point at the top or an open part at the top. If you make it with an open top, that part points up, and we won't worry about it. Hold your pencil hand flat, and point your thumb down, The *bottom* open part of the 4 should match the opening between your thumb and your fingers.

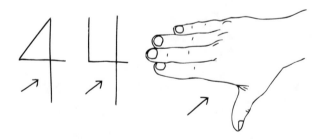

A 5 has a round open part, and a squarish one. Look at the round open part. It should be the same as your pencil hand.

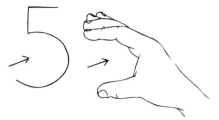

Whoops! Remember, "Sixes Don't Fit," so the 6 should be the other way. (If you can't be sure it's the other way, check it with your *other* hand).

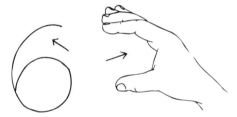

A 7 is just one big open part. Put your pencil hand flat, with the thumb down. The open part between your thumb and fingers should match the 7.

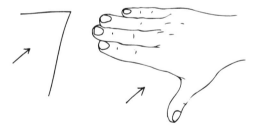

The 9 has a funny-shaped open part, but it should match your pencil hand, too.

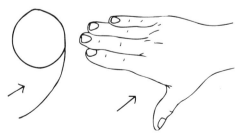

At first, you may want to use this method just when you've written a numeral, and you're not sure if it's right or not. Later, maybe you will want to use it *before* you write. Pretty soon, you'll have practiced doing it right so many times that you probably won't need to check any more at all!

Studying with Rhythm or Music

Another great way to study is with rhythm. Maybe you already do this sometimes. Many people find counting on their fingers easier if they tap a certain way, like on the ends of their noses!

If you have things to memorize, foot tapping or hand clapping just might help. You can tap the desk top, drum fashion, as you recite or read the material you have to learn. Auditory learners seem to learn from the *sound* of the tapping; perhaps the visual learners get it from *seeing* and *doing*.

Both finger-counting and rhythm learning are bound to raise some eyebrows. If you go all out on the tapping and thumping while studying in your room, you may have a lot of explaining to do to your parents! If you share a room with a sister or brother, this method won't be too popular either.

Some suggestions for making up rap songs to learn material were included in the section for auditory learners. Because rap is so much fun, even visual learners might enjoy trying it. Since it's not a very visual approach, however, a visual learner should move on to another idea if rap doesn't work for him or her.

Using Texture to Learn

Another interesting method that some auditory *and* visual learners may find useful is "finger-writing on texture." You may have seen or used sandpaper letters, which you trace with a fingertip to help you remember how it *feels* to form a certain letter. Perhaps you even learned to write this way. If it worked then, why not use it now? You can practice "writing" with a fingertip on any rough surface, and the action you use in forming the word may help you remember it.

This book's first "junior editorial consultant" found that to practice writing her spelling words with a fingertip on her blue-jeaned leg worked well, especially when she didn't have a pencil and paper handy for her visual learning style.

Clean Desk for a Clear Mind!

First, it's true – you *will* be able to work and learn better if you clear off and clean off your desk first. If all those books, pencils, scratch pads, and assorted junk aren't right in front of you, they can't distract you. So clear up that desk.

Don't over-do, though! Sometimes when I have work that I *really* am putting off, I spend as much time as I can tidying my desk and sharpening all my pencils three or four times! I'm only kidding myself when I do that, though. Clean up quickly, and then get started working.

If there's too much junk to take care of, and you find yourself getting frustrated, ask one of your parents to help you get everything sorted out – maybe not immediately, but how about this weekend? You will want to throw away as much junk as possible, too.

You may find that you need more storage space. Maybe some of those storage cubes would help. You can put all the things you need to take to school tomorrow in one of them. Then when you come home, always put your books right there, so they'll be ready at homework time. You can make up for a disorganized mind by having an organized system!

Distractions

If you find that when you read or write in a workbook, you are distracted even by what's on the other page, try putting a blank sheet of paper over the page you're not using. It can help a lot and makes a good bookmark, too.

Some books are printed on thin paper, so that the printing on the next page shows through. A piece of *black* paper *under* the page you're reading or working on helps cure this problem at once – try it!

If you're distracted more by what you *hear* than what you *see*, (and what distracts you doesn't necessarily match which way you learn best, either) you still need a tidy desk. (All the junk rattling around can be noisy, too.) And *turn off* the radio, stereo, or TV if you find yourself listening or watching and letting your homework just sit there – it won't do itself, you know!

Some kids feel that they can work better with music playing. Maybe it helps cover up the noises from a busy family in the rest of the house or street noises from outside. You're going to have to be pretty honest with yourself – does it *really* cover up the outside noise, or do you just like to listen to it? Can you *really* study better with it on, or does it distract you? If it helps – great. If not, be honest with yourself and turn it off.

Television is another matter. Almost nobody can study better with the television on. The best way to deal with television when you're studying is not to have it on. There is a way to *use* television to help you study quickly and efficiently, though, and that's to use it as a reward for yourself.

Rewarding Yourself

Television seems to be so addictive to kids and adults that it's easy to get trapped by it and to forget all the important things you have to do. If you use it properly, though, it can be a help. To do this, pick out something that you'd really like to watch and make a deal with yourself: "This show comes on in 50 minutes. I'll set the timer for 50 minutes. If I've finished this much work before it rings, I get to watch the show." If you still have more homework after the show, then it's back to work!

You can use an alarm clock for a timer, or a small wind-up

kitchen timer if you have one. If you aren't very good at setting an alarm clock, ask your folks to get one of the kitchen timers. They cost about ten dollars, and there are many good uses for them, as we'll see later.

It's a good idea to let your parents in on the reward idea ahead of time and get their approval. If you don't, you might be asked, "Have you finished *all* your homework?" and not be allowed to watch television if you haven't! And remember – after the show is over, back to work until the next reward time you set for yourself.

You'll have to experiment to find out how long you should be able to work without a break. Ask your parents or your teacher if you're not sure. Some people may want to work for short periods, such as about 20 minutes, and then take a break for a cookie or a drink, or maybe for a five-minute bike ride around the block or a short phone call to a friend. It wouldn't be smart to study for 15 minutes and then take a half-hour break for a television show!

Many activities make nice rewards. Usually, something quite different from sitting in one spot doing homework is helpful. That's why riding a bike, in-line skating, just walking or running, or some other physical activity are especially good. If the weather's bad or those activities aren't acceptable for some other reason, video or computer games might work. A special problem with them is the time factor! Some video games or computer games last for a *very* long time. Since you don't know exactly how long a game will last, it's hard to schedule your reward exactly. How about setting a limit of one game, and make sure it's one that won't last too long? Remember, these games are a little addictive, too – you'll have to play fair with yourself, and get back to the homework before your next reward period!

You can use the timer to help you do other chores, too. Any time you can play a game with yourself ("Can I get this done before the timer rings?") it's a lot easier not to waste time! Your parents might want to try it on jobs they don't like to do. Maybe your dad would enjoy setting a challenge for himself, such as "If I get the recycling stuff collected and hauled out to the curb before the timer rings, I'll shoot a few baskets with the kid!" You can even suggest the idea to your brothers or sisters for their homework.

Remembering Things

Lots of people who *don't* have learning disabilities have trouble remembering things, but it seems to be a real problem for those of us with learning disabilities. You have already learned in Chapter Four that if you're a visual learner, you remember things better if you *see* them. If you're an auditory learner, you remember better what you *hear*. Here are a couple of memory boosters that might help, whichever way you learn best.

I'm sure you've heard people say, "Tie a string around your finger so you won't forget!" What they mean is, give yourself some kind of *physical* hint to remind you that there is something you need to remember.

Suppose you have trouble remembering to take your clean gym clothes to school on Mondays. A way to help you remember is to make them impossible to forget – arrange things so they'll remind themselves!

Here's how. On Sunday night, hang them on your bedroom doorknob (or the doorknob of the door you always go out for school, if your parents will let you) so that you have to *touch* them in order to get the door open. If that's not strong enough, prop them against the door so that they'll fall over on your foot when you open the door!

Of course, to make this work, you have to get things ready the night before. And that's an important hint for people who have trouble remembering – start far ahead of time. As soon as you remember you're going to have to do something later, do something about it right away. If you remember you're going to need money for a field trip, go ask your parents *then*, or write a note about it and put it wherever your family leaves messages for each other. (If your family doesn't have such a place, there's no better time than right now to start one!)

When you go back and forth from home to school or a job every day, it's important to have one place to keep everything that needs to go with you. Most kids have a backpack and a locker at school. The backpack comes home with you, but what happens to the things in it? You usually don't have a locker at home, but a whole room! Sometimes you may get to school, and discover that you left your homework on your desk, or somewhere else at home.

Maybe you *do* need a locker at home – or at least, one place where all your school things go as soon as your homework is done. If you have brothers or sisters, each one of you needs a place. Maybe it can be a shelf by the kitchen door or even in the laundry room by the garage. Maybe a stack of those plastic boxes made like old-fashioned milk crates, a different color for each of you, would be just right. Talk to your parents about it if remembering things is a problem at your house.

Another memory trick that can help you more than you think is to be careful how you program your mind about remembering. Your mind is like a computer, and it will do what you tell it to do. Tell yourself what you need to remember, and word it positively – *don't* word it in such a way that you're telling yourself you might forget! Do it this way:

Say: "I *will* remember to drop off that book at the library!"

Not: "I hope I don't forget to drop off that book at the library!"

and *never*: "I bet I'll forget to drop off that book at the library."

Doorknob reminders are great, too. You can use some of those little yellow sticky-notes, or just paper and tape. Stick a small reminder right on the doorknob, so that you can't possibly open the door without your hand's touching it. It's pretty hard to ignore that way! Even auditory learners, who can walk right past a foot-high, bright pink sign, can't miss these.

It's not just people with learning disabilities who have problems remembering. People used to get dead batteries in their cars by turning on the lights on dark mornings, and forgetting to turn them off later when it was light out. Now some cars have automatic timers that turn them off, and almost all other cars have some sort of a beeper or buzzer that sounds when the keys are removed if the lights are still on. Cars remind you when you forget your safety belts, too.

Mnemonics

There are some special tricks and other ways to help you remember things. These are called *mnemonics,* or *mnemonic devices.* (That's pronounced "nee-*mon*-ick," and most grownups say it wrong!) They're just little ways to help your brain put a structure to things so that they stay together and are easier to remember. They're *not* cheating – they're just smarter ways to study and remember.

One kind of mnemonic device that makes a good way to study if you have to learn lists of things is to make up silly words called *acronyms.* In an acronym, each letter stands for the first letter of the things you have to remember.

For example, one of the most famous acronyms is HOMES, for remembering the names of the five Great Lakes – **H**uron, **O**ntario, **M**ichigan, **E**rie, and **S**uperior. I can't remember them without the acronym. To remember which one is which is harder. I can remember that Lake Superior is the top one, higher than the others, because I know that *superior* means "best or highest." But what about the other ones? For that, I need a **SM**all **HE**lp, **O**h! That gives me the order: First Superior, then Michigan, then Huron, then Erie, and finally Ontario. Got it!

Sometimes silly sentences work well. They're easier for auditory learners than for visual learners, but even visual learners can use them.

For example, in 8th or 9th grade science, you have to learn the scientific classification system for living things, the taxonomy. A very old memory device is the sentence "**K**ing **P**hilip **C**ame **O**ver from **G**reece to **S**pain." You have to remember to skip the unimportant words, but this sentence helps you remember **K**ingdom, **Ph**ylum, **C**lass, **O**rder, **G**enus, and **S**pecies. (If you don't know what all of that means yet, don't worry. You'll get it in science later – and you'll already know how to remember the names, in order!)

Another good mnemonic is for remembering the names of the planets, in order, starting with the one closest to the sun: **M**ary's **V**iolet **E**yes **M**ake **J**ohn **S**it **U**p **N**ights **P**roposing! (Some people prefer **M**y **V**ery **E**ducated **M**other **J**ust **S**erved **U**s **N**ine **P**izzas.) So what does it mean? Well, there are two m's, Mercury and Mars, but it's easy to remember that *Mercury comes first* – after all, isn't that the stuff in a thermometer that tells you how hot it is? And isn't it pretty hot close to the sun? So try it: **M**ercury, **V**enus, **E**arth, **M**ars, **J**upiter, **S**aturn, **U**ranus, **N**eptune, **P**luto!

Try making up your own mnemonics – the sillier the better.

Homework Charts

If a problem for you is knowing what homework you're

supposed to do when you get home, make yourself a homework chart. If you just have one teacher, it's pretty easy. Just take a piece of paper, and divide it into five sections, one for each day of the week, and write the days at the top. At school, write down the assignments as the teacher gives them to you. Keep the chart in the front of your notebook, so it's easy to find. If you aren't sure you got an assignment right, ask the teacher to look at it just before you leave and add anything you forgot. Make sure you have all the books you need in your backpack, and you're all set!

If you have several teachers, make a separate section of the daily part for each teacher. Then put the assignments down as you get them. Again, any time you're not sure if you got it right, ask the teacher to check it over. Most teachers will be glad to help when they see how responsible you're being.

Long-term homework, such as a report or science fair project, takes more planning. Let's say you have a book report to do in two weeks. Divide up the steps, and decide when you're going to do each one. Maybe you want to (1) have the book picked out by Friday, (2) do a lot of the reading over the first weekend, (3) finish up during the week, (4) write the book report over the second weekend – whoops, you'll need a folder to put it in! Go back and put "Buy folder" as one of the tasks you'll do on that first weekend while you're doing a lot of the reading. Can you see how breaking it up into parts, ahead of time, can keep you from having to ask your parents to run to the store for a folder late one night, or having to stop at a convenience store in the morning?

This is the same kind of thinking you need to do for any long-term project. You have to start *further* ahead for something as major as a science fair project, of course!

A Final Word About Studying

It's important for you to take charge of yourself about studying. You're setting some habits for yourself that you'll have many years from now when you're the grownup. You'll be able to use your good study habits to help your own children!

To get the best out of yourself, remember that you're going to have to put the best in. Keep yourself healthy – that means plenty of sleep, eating and drinking the right things, keeping clean, and saving time to have fun, too.

Getting plenty of sleep is a very important part of taking care of yourself. Some people seem to need only a few hours of sleep. Others are cross as bears without ten hours! Let your own body's reactions guide you and your parents to picking your bedtime, no matter what age you are. You may decide that 8:30's your bedtime, even if your kid brother stays up until 9:00.

Some people are cheerful in the morning; others are grouches and are slow to get moving. If you're a morning slowpoke, it's especially important for you to get everything set the night before.

If even getting yourself dressed is an unpleasant chore, don't expect to be able to do last-minute studying or organizing your books then!

A Final Note

Maybe some of these ideas will work for you. If you have some other ideas that work better – use them! Maybe some of the ideas in this chapter won't work for you, but will give you some ideas of your own. That's the important thing – each person is different, and instead of fumbling around with someone else's ideas that don't work, set a goal of working out the best ways for *you*.

Chapter Seven

All About ADD

A big bunch of problems that some kids with learning disabilities have, and some lucky ones don't have are sometimes called *ADD* or *ADHD*. Those initials are short for Attention Deficit Disorder, or Attention Deficit Hyperactivity Disorder.

What that means is that a person with ADD or ADHD has trouble with certain things, such as paying attention for very long, sitting (or standing) still, or thinking before talking or doing something. These are three things that most of the experts mean when they say ADD or ADHD, but there are some others. Luckily, not too many people have *all* of these problems!

Nobody knows for sure what causes these problems, just as nobody seems to know what causes learning disabilities. Some experts say these problems are caused by something different going on in the brain that's permanent and won't change. Some experts say that there are many things that can cause these problems, such as allergies and other kinds of physical problems. The main thing is that kids with learning disabilities seem to have these problems more often than kids without learning disabilities.

Let's look at what these problems are, and you can decide if you have trouble in these areas. After each problem, we'll look at some ideas that might help. You may want to try some of your own ideas, too, once you know what the problems are.

Trouble with Paying Attention

There are several different ways you can have trouble with paying attention. Some people just have trouble paying attention to one thing or one activity for very long at a time. That's called *short attention span.* If you have this problem, you may be able to do very well at something as long as you don't have to work at it for very long. Then you may start having trouble keeping your mind on what you're supposed to be doing, or getting fidgety.

The funny thing about this problem is that sometimes, you might be able to pay attention to some things for a *very* long time if it's something you are really, really interested in and that you are good at. Maybe you can sit for hours playing computer games, or watching your favorite TV programs. Then your teacher or your parents may think that you really could pay attention to your schoolwork better if you would try.

Sometimes this problem makes a person get lower grades. This is because even though you may get everything right at the beginning, if the work time is too long, you may start to make too many "careless" mistakes (at least, that's what the teacher calls them). Or if the teacher takes a long time to explain something, your attention span may run out, and you may miss the last part of the explanation.

If you have a short attention span, perhaps you or your parents can talk to your teacher about making sure that you are able to do your work in short periods of time, with breaks in between. When you do your homework, you might want to set a timer, and work for a little while. Then take a break to enjoy a snack, or to listen to one song on the radio, or just walk around the house once. Then go back and work some more.

You will probably get more done in an hour even if you take a little break every so often, because you will be working with a fresh attention span. Be sure to let your parents know what you are doing, so that they won't think you are just putting off getting your work done! If you think you may forget to go back to work, ask someone to remind you, or set your timer for the few minutes of break you need. When it rings, it's back to work for you!

It also may help if you don't do all the same kinds of work at one time. You might work on reading for a while, and then color the maps you have to do for social studies. Then you might do your chores, like taking out the garbage. Then you might go back and do some more reading. Just don't try to do all your reading at one time, and then all your writing, and so on. Changing to a different kind of work every few minutes makes it more interesting, too.

Another kind of attention problem is paying *too much* attention. If that sounds strange, maybe it is. With this problem, you might be watching TV, and you don't know your mother is calling you until she is practically screaming at you. Or you might be working on a math problem (or whispering to a friend) and not notice the teacher walking up the aisle toward you.

This problem may be more rare than not being able to pay attention long enough. Some people think this wouldn't be a problem at all – think how hard you could concentrate, they say! But it *is* a problem if you need to be able to pay attention to several things within a short period of time. You need to be able to turn your attention to new jobs when it's time to work on them.

This is a hard problem to work on. Usually, you need help from other people in working around this one. Your teacher or your parents (or your friends) will have to know that they may have to touch you to get your attention. They will also have to remember that you don't hear anything they say, or notice what they are doing, until they get your attention shifted from what you were doing before to what they want you to see or hear.

Big Upsets over Little Things

Do you get mad or upset all of a sudden over every little thing? If you do, you may have this problem. It just means that you react to anything that goes wrong as if it were a great disaster. Later, it may seem silly that you got so upset. You may get upset and cry too easily, or you may get mad and even want to hit or kick.

This can be a tough problem to solve on your own, too. When you are at home, you can have your parents help you find some way to work things out when you get upset. Maybe you can go off by yourself and listen to music for a while. Maybe you will want to shoot a few baskets in the back yard, or find a pillow you can punch a few times. It may be harder to deal with in school, where getting up and walking out might get you in trouble. Maybe you can talk to your teacher for permission ahead of time.

Try to think of something to tell yourself when you feel yourself getting upset. Make up your own reminder, and use it every time you are feeling that something is more important than it really is. Maybe you will want to say, "Is this really important?" or "Is this worth getting upset about?" What I tell myself is, "There are more important things than this in my life!" It works for me – not always, but most of the time.

Distractibility

Another kind of problem is called *distractibility*. This means that even though you are paying attention to what's going on, if something else happens, you find yourself paying attention to that instead of being able to keep your mind where it's supposed to be. (You can see why some experts think that distractibility is just another kind of attention problem.)

Some people are more distracted by things they see, such as other people moving around the classroom, fancy bulletin boards, or maybe decorations hanging from the ceiling. Other people are more bothered by things they hear, such as other people talking while they're trying to work, or noise from next door or down the hall.

If you have the problem of distractibility, think about what kinds of things distract you. Is it what you see? We might call that *sight distractibility*. If so, try to get your teacher to let you sit somewhere in the classroom where there is not so much going on, and where you can see him or her without people in between. You definitely don't want to sit facing the window that looks out towards the physical education field! When you study at home, work in a clear area, perhaps facing a wall. Don't try to study and watch TV at the same time!

If you have *sound distractibility,* you are more bothered by what you hear. I have this problem – I can't think or solve problems very well if there are some kinds of sounds around me. The sound of people talking is the worst distraction for me. As a teacher, I have to be sure my students are not talking when they are supposed to be listening, or I can't even make my sentences come out right.

You will want to study in a quiet place, maybe in your own room, rather than in the same room with your brothers and sisters, or in the kitchen when one of your parents is fixing dinner or doing the dishes. Some people can use soft music to cover up outside noise to help them concentrate – this often helps me. Other people may find just the opposite – if music is playing, they keep listening to it instead of working on what they need to get done. You might even try studying with a pair of old stereo headphones on to block out noise.

With some experimenting, you can work out a good solution for yourself at home. At school, sitting near the front of the room can help. Usually, people are less likely to talk when they're near the teacher, so they won't be distracting you, either.

Mood Swings

This is another problem that sometimes goes along with ADD. One minute you feel fine; the next minute you feel awful. Sometimes your mood changes all of a sudden, and it seems that nothing at all happened to make it change.

If you're a teenager, it might help to know that mood swings are pretty normal for *all* teens, not just those with ADD or learning disabilities. If you're a pre-teen, maybe this is just one way you'll be more ready for your teen years than someone else! I know that probably doesn't help too much.

Sometimes it helps to remind yourself, when you're feeling awful, that in a little while, things will be back to normal again. I like to listen to my favorite happy music when I feel bad, or call up a friend I can just talk to. Some people even like to go in another room and just cry for a few minutes! Others like to go kick a ball around, or sit and cuddle a pet. When you find something that makes you feel better, remember it, so you can use it again next time you're feeling low.

Being "Hyper"

If you're "hyper," you've probably been hearing about it for a long time. The real term is *hyperactivity*. It just means being more active than most people of your age. If you are hyper, people always seem to be telling you to sit still, or stand still, or to quit fidgeting.

You may need less sleep than other kids your age, or you may need more. Often, kids who are hyperactive are either all the way awake, or fast asleep, with not much time in between. You may wake up almost instantly in the morning. If your parents or your brothers and sisters wake up more slowly, they may seem very grouchy and slow-moving in the morning, and probably get more upset at you at that time. When you were small, you may have had to be carried to bed often because you fell asleep all of a sudden while you were still in the family room watching TV.

The big problem, though, if you are hyperactive, is that you are constantly moving, and other people just don't seem to understand why you are always on the go. Even when you try to sit still, you may be jiggling, or swinging your feet, or tapping on something.

Hyperactivity is another problem that's hard to take care of on your own. Some people find that it helps them to get plenty of *very* active exercise – running, biking, or roller-blading, maybe. Other people find that too much activity just seems to wind them up even more. You will have to see what works best for you.

Some people take medicine for hyperactivity. Ritalin is one very common medication that is used. It may help a person be much less hyperactive, and it may also help with many of the other ADD problems we have been talking about. If your doctor has prescribed medicine for you, be sure you take it just as the doctor ordered. You and your parents shouldn't make any changes without checking with the doctor.

If you have problems with hyperactivity and are not taking medication for it, you might ask your parents if they have talked to your doctor about medicine to help you. There may be some reason why they have not, or they may have thought you would not want to take it. It isn't right for everyone, but for certain people, it can be very helpful.

Acting or Talking Without Thinking

Doing something or saying something without taking time to think first is called *impulsivity*. It can get you into all sorts of trouble, and it can embarrass you sometimes.

If you have this problem in speech, this means that you often say just whatever pops into your head. Then sometimes you're sorry you said anything at all! You may say something angry and then find out that the person you're mad at didn't really do or say what you thought he or she did. Now you're sorry, and you might even have made your friend mad at you.

Maybe you often do things quickly, without thinking first. When you were little, you might have been likely to run out into the street after a ball or a pet without looking to see if any cars were coming. Now, you may jump up to do something and knock someone or something down. Spills and accidents just always seem to happen to you.

This may be a hard problem to handle because it happens to you *before* you have time to think. The only way to deal with it is to train yourself to count – oh, maybe to 3 – before you follow an idea with words or action. You have to train yourself to do it *every* time, or you won't be ready to do it when it's really important. People won't mind if it takes you a minute to answer or do something. They would rather you do it right!

Doing Things Over and Over

Doing things over and over, even if it doesn't do any good, is *perseveration.* It's not the same thing as *perseverance*; that means trying and trying until you get it right! *Perseveration* has you even doing the same wrong thing again and again. If you have this problem, you may find that you might start scribbling on the edge of your paper, or re-tracing a word you already wrote. Then, before you even know it, you have marked the whole thing up. Or you start chewing on your pencil, or a fingernail, or tearing up little bits of paper, and soon you've made a terrible mess.

You may have this problem in talking, too. That's when a person just can't seem to stop talking. If you have this, sometimes even your best friend or your grandmother may say, "Can't you just hush up for five minutes?"

To work on perseveration problems, first figure out whether your problem is doing, talking, or both. If it's doing, figure out when it is the most trouble for you. If you often perseverate in marking up your papers or workbooks, try working with a piece of extra paper near you. When you stop to think when you are working, train yourself to scribble or mark on the extra paper, not the good sheet or workbook page that you will have to turn in. Your teachers will be glad when they see that you are turning in neater work!

Sometimes having messy papers to begin with can start a person perseverating. When you take out a piece of notebook paper, take it out carefully; don't tear it out. If you tear it, those torn parts may start your fingers tearing just a little more, and a little more, and you'll soon have a mess.

Many children and teens with ADD seem to bite their fingernails. In many cases, it's a perseveration problem rather than just a regular habit. If a fingernail breaks or feels rough, you may start to bite it – and one nibble leads to more if perseveration is one of your problems! Clipping or filing a fingernail when it starts to break, and not even *starting* to bite it, is a way to keep from nibbling until your fingertips hurt and you have no fingernails left at all. When your were small, your parents may have put nasty-tasting stuff on your fingernails to keep you from biting them. It probably didn't work. If you decide you want to try it for yourself, though, just so you'll notice when you start to bite, it probably *will* help you.

Other Problems

You may have some other sorts of behaviors that your doctor, teachers, or parents think is part of an ADD or ADHD problem. You can ask someone you trust if there are some others you might want to work on. See if you can work out ideas for yourself to solve them, or if friends with the same problems can help you. Sometimes your teacher or a counselor can make suggestions, too.

Which brings up another thing. All of these problems, plus the problems in school subjects that are a part of learning disabilities, are sometimes very hard to live with. Sometimes you get very frustrated. Sometimes you get angry. Sometimes you may feel sad or depressed.

These feelings are pretty normal, but they are no fun to deal with all by yourself. It's okay to say that you want some help working on them. You can talk to your school counselor, or let your parents know that you'd like to have some special help working on feelings. There are many nice things about talking to a counselor, and one of the nicest is that you can talk about *anything* that is bothering you, and it's just between you and the counselor.

So if you can handle your problems on your own, that's okay. But it's also okay to ask for help.

Chapter Eight

"I've got people problems, too!"

After you've gone through the big chore of finding out about yourself and facing up to your problem (which wasn't as bad as all the things you imagined it could be!), you still have to face the problems that other people can cause you.

Sometimes people can cause you problems when they're really trying to help, but they just don't understand. Often they think they know what the problem is, but they've got the wrong answer – just as you did when you thought you were dumb!

You get tired of hearing people say that you don't try or that you don't care. You're sick of people blaming you for something that's not your fault, or blaming your parents, as though you were a "bad kid" and you and they were both to blame. And the people who go overboard the other way, thinking you're not as smart as you really are, are a real pain.

Maybe you can strike a blow for yourself and lots of other kids with learning disabilities, too, if you can educate these people. You've already started educating the most important one – yourself. Now let's see what you can do with the rest of the world!

Why not start with the ones who really care about you, but who can't always understand what it's like to be smart but to have trouble learning – your own parents. If you have brothers or sisters who sometimes give you a bad time, and who can't understand why some things are hard for you, you'll *definitely* want to try some of these tricks on them. Your parents can help you after you have had them try some of these things.

To do this, I'm going to share some of my "trade secrets" with you. I travel around the country doing a special workshop for parents or for teachers that helps them understand what a learning disability feels like. I have been doing this for more years than you are old, so I know it really works!

I use games and tricks to make easy things hard for my audiences; and I'm going to teach you how to use some of my sneaky tricks (but not all of them – I've got to have *some* secrets!) to help your parents, or your teachers, or even some of your friends see what learning with a learning disability feels like.

Here's a good one I learned as a party game – guaranteed to frustrate dads, especially.

Draw a simple design on a piece of paper. You can use the design below, or make up your own. A dollar sign is a good one, but you can make any design that doesn't have mostly straight lines. Even just a random scrawl will work well.

Cover the design with a piece of tracing paper, and put a mirror on the table, so that your dad can see the design in the mirror. (If you don't have tracing paper, just have him use a colored fine-point marker to trace your original drawing.) Then hold a piece of cardboard in front of him so that he *can't* see the paper, except in the mirror. Now ask him to trace the design.

He's in for quite a surprise! He'll be able to see the design, and to know where he wants the pencil to go, but he'll have a hard time doing it. It will be as hard for him as writing is for kids with some kinds of learning problems. His hand will get tired, and his paper may end up *very* messy. Maybe it will be easier for him to see why you get upset when you have to copy something over, and your hand is already tired, or why some of your papers are pretty messy!

For this next stunt, you can use the story on page 99 just as it is in the book, or you can make a photocopy of it. Just ask your "victim" to read it aloud. (Be sure he or she doesn't turn the paper over and hold it up to the light!) For some kids with learning disabilities, some or all of the letters in a word may seem to get turned around that way. Maybe it was that way for you.

Another reading trick is to copy a long paragraph or a story, putting in X's instead of vowels.

Xf yxx trxxd tx txll sxmxxnx hxw hxrd xt xs tx hxvx x lxxrnxng dxsxbxlxty, hx xr shx wxxld hxvx x hxrd txmx xndxrstxndxng. Whxn x pxrsxn cxn rxxd xxsxly, xr rxmxmbxr xxsxly, xt's hxrd tx xmxgxnx whxt xt xs lxkx tx

hxvx prxblxms dxxng sxmx vxry sxmplx thxngs. Xnx
rxxsxn thxsx trxcks xrx sx mxch fxn fxr thxsx xf xs wxth
lxxrnxng dxsxbxlxtxxs xs thxt xt gxvxs xs x chxncx tx shxw
xthxr pxxplx whxt wx gx thrxxgh, xvxry dxy xn schxxl xnd
xn xxr lxvxs. Mxybx xf mxrx pxxplx hxd x chxncx tx sxx
hxw hxrd wx hxvx tx wxrk tx lxxrn, thxy wxxld bx mxrx
xndxrstxndxng.

*(To see how this looks with the vowels in their proper places,
see Sample A on page 102.)*

Another way is to *leave out* all of the vowels. Just take any
simple story, and type it on the computer without the vowels, this
way:

Mny ppl jst thnk tht ppl wth lrnng dsblts r lzy, r tht w
dn't try vry hrd. Thy d nt rlz tht w hv t wrk hrd t pyng ttntn
vry sngl mnt f th dy f w wnt t lrn. W cn't jst lrn thngs frm
hvng thm hppn rnd s; w hv t fcs ll r ttntn t lrn. W rn't dmb;
w'r s smrt s th vrg, r vn smrtr. Whn w chv, w knw tht ll r
ffrts wr wrthwhl, nd w rmmbr th ppl wh ncrgd s.

*(To see how this looks with all the vowels put back, see Sample
B on page 102.)*

Try this out on your "victims." You can probably think of lots
of ways to show reading problems. Just having them read a story
with the d's, b's, p's, g's, and q's (the letters so many kids with
learning disabilities have trouble with) switched around is great
fun. It's even harder if you also put spaces here and there in the
middle of words and skip a few spaces where they should be, like
this:

Som etimesi tis ver ybiffic ulttok eed work ingharp
whe nbeogled onot seemt ore alize tha tyou ar ereal ly
try ind. I tis enco urabing toknowa dout famo us deodle
who haved eens uccess fulins bite oft heirl earn inb
bisad ili ties. Wins ton chur chill, ne Ison Roc kef eller,

98

The Story of the Three Bears and Goldilocks

There were once three bears who lived in a little cottage in the woods. There were Papa Bear, Mama Bear, and Baby Bear. One day Mama Bear made some nice porridge. But when the three bears tasted the porridge, it was too hot! So they decided to take a walk in the woods while it cooled.

While they were gone, who should come along but Goldilocks. She knocked on the door. When no one answered, she went in. She saw the porridge on the table, and tasted the big bowl.

"Ooh!" she said. "This porridge is too hot!"

She tasted the second bowl, but it was too cold. The third bowl was just right, so she ate it all up. Then she went into the sitting room, and saw three chairs. She sat in the big chair.

"Ooh!" she said. "This chair is too hard!"

She sat in the second chair, but it was too soft. The third chair was just right, but she broke it to smithereens! Then she went upstairs, and saw three beds. She lay down in the big bed.

"Ooh!" she said. "This bed is too hard!"

She lay in the second bed, and it was too soft. The third bed was just right, and she fell asleep at once.

The three bears returned home from their walk.

"Somebody's been eating my porridge!" said Papa Bear.

"Somebody's been eating my porridge!" said Mama Bear.

"Somebody's been eating my porridge," said Baby Bear, "and ate it all up!"

The bears went in the sitting room.

"Somebody's been sitting in my chair!" said Papa Bear.

"Somebody's been sitting in my chair!" said Mama Bear.

"Somebody's been sitting in my chair," said Baby Bear, "and smashed it all to smithereens!"

The bears went upstairs.

"Somebody's been sleeping in my bed!" said Papa Bear.

"Somebody's been sleeping in my bed!" said Mama Bear.

"Somebody's been sleeping in my bed," said Baby Bear, "and here she is!"

With that, Goldilocks woke up with a start, saw the three bears, jumped out of bed, ran all the way home, and never went back again. The three bears, of course, lived happily ever after.

The End

George Pat ton, Cher, Bruce Jenner, anb Tom Cruise are goo gex ambles of geog lewhos elive shave enco uradeg otherd eogl ewith lear nind disad ili ties.

(To see how this looks without reversals and strange spaces, see Sample C on page 102.)

You can try a math game, too. Tell your victim that you are going to change the rules for math. Say that the "+" sign means subtract, the "÷" sign means multiply, the "-" sign means divide, and the "x" sign means add. Then write a long, *easy* problem down for him or her to work, like:

$$6 + 2 \div 1 \times 4 =$$

Bet he or she can't get the right answer! (I *think* the answer is 8, but I've even confused myself!)

Another one that's especially good for a group, such as your whole family or a class, is to play a special game of "Simon Says." (You remember that in "Simon Says," the leader gives directions such as "Take three steps forward" or "Raise your right hand," but you are *not* supposed to follow the instructions unless the leader says "Simon Says" first.) In *this* version of "Simon Says," all the instructions are reversed! When the leader says "left," that means "right;" when the leader says "forward," it means "backward." This will be harder for your group than they think. They have to remember to reverse all the instructions, *and* be sure not to do anything unless you say "Simon Says" first. This is how hard it is for some kids with learning disabilities to get complicated instructions right.

These are good activities for helping people understand learning disabilities. Sometimes in my workshops I have had parents really understand their son's or daughter's problems for the first time. One father had talked to me for a long time. He felt that his son, Larry, just didn't try hard enough, and that "learning disability" was just an excuse. He loved his son, but he just couldn't see why this very smart boy had so much trouble learning. The man finally tried the mirror drawing trick. He worked and worked. He smudged the paper, broke the pencil (and I think he may even have said one or two words he shouldn't have). When he finished, you couldn't even recognize the design. He looked at it for a very long time, and shook his head. He seemed to be talking to himself when he said very quietly, "Don't yell at Larry; don't yell at Larry."

If it helped Larry, maybe it'll help you, too.

That's about it. Now you know what your problems are, how to work around them, and how to help people understand you better. Your part of this book is just about finished! The next part of the book may be a special treat, though. It will give you lots of "homework" – but not for *you* to do yourself! It's homework to assign to your parents and teachers!

What they'll find in the rest of the book is a nice long list of some things that might be helpful for them to read – some other books that will help them understand learning disabilities, and what to do about them, and some books on things related to learning disabilities that might be helpful. There are also some books that are good for kids to read about ADD, medication, and some other problems. That list starts on page 121, so you can take a look at it yourself. If you see a book you'd like to read, ask your folks or your teacher to locate it for you.

There are also letters to your teacher and your parents. I wrote them to tell them some of the kinds of things that kids like you have told me they want their parents and teachers to know – some of the things it may be hard for you to say to them. You might want to look at those letters and underline or use a highlighter marker to mark anything you want them to pay special attention to. Then, in the blank section at the end of each letter, marked "P.S.," write for yourself anything you think maybe I left out. You can sign the letters, too, if you want to.

You can look the rest of the book over, of course, and look at some of the books and ideas I am suggesting to your teachers and parents. You might want to pick out and mark things you think they need to find out about – or just turn the whole job over to them.

Sample A

If you tried to tell someone how hard it is to have a learning disability, he or she would have a hard time understanding. When a person can read easily, or remember easily, it's hard to imagine what it is like to have problems doing some very simple things. One reason these tricks are so much fun for those of us with learning disabilities is that it gives us a chance to show other people what we go through, every day in school and in our lives. Maybe if more people had a chance to see how hard we have to work to learn, they would be more understanding.

Sample B

Many people just think that people with learning disabilities are lazy, or that we don't try very hard. They do not realize that we have to work hard at paying attention every single minute of the day if we want to learn. We can't just learn things from having them happen around us; we have to focus all our attention to learn, we aren't dumb; we're as smart as the average, or even smarter. When we achieve, we know that all our efforts were worthwhile, and we remember the people who encouraged us.

Sample C

Sometimes it is very difficult to keep working hard when people do not seem to realize that you are really trying. It is encouraging to know about famous people who have been successful in spite of their learning disabilities. Winston Churchill, Nelson Rockefeller, George Patton, Cher, Bruce Jenner, and Tom Cruise are good examples of people whose lives have encouraged other people with learning disabilities.

The Story of the Three Bears and Goldilocks

There were once three bears who lived in a little cottage in the woods. There were Papa Bear, Mama Bear, and Baby Bear.

One day Mama Bear made some nice porridge. But when the three bears tasted the porridge, it was too hot! So they decided to take a walk in the woods while it cooled.

While they were gone, who should come along but Goldilocks. She knocked on the door. When no one answered, she went in. She saw the porridge on the table, and tasted the big bowl.

"Ooh!" she said. "This porridge is too hot!"

She tasted the second bowl, but it was too cold. The third bowl was just right, so she ate it all up. Then she went into the sitting room, and saw three chairs. She sat in the big chair.

"Ooh!" she said. "This chair is too hard!"

She sat in the second chair, but it was too soft. The third chair was just right, but she broke it to smithereens! Then she went upstairs, and saw three beds. She lay down in the big bed.

"Ooh!" she said. "This bed is too hard!"

She lay in the second bed, and it was too soft. The third bed was just right, and she fell asleep at once.

The three bears returned home from their walk.

"Somebody's been eating my porridge!" said Papa Bear.

"Somebody's been eating *my* porridge!" said Mama Bear.

"Somebody's been eating my porridge," said Baby Bear, "and ate it all up!"

The bears went in the sitting room.

"Somebody's been sitting in my chair!" said Papa Bear.

"Somebody's been sitting in *my* chair!" said Mama Bear.

"Somebody's been sitting in my chair," said Baby Bear, "and smashed it all to smithereens!"

The bears went upstairs.

"Somebody's been sleeping in my bed!" said Papa Bear.

"Somebody's been sleeping in *my* bed!" said Mama Bear.

"Somebody's been sleeping in my bed," said Baby Bear, "and here she is!"

With that, Goldilocks woke up with a start, saw the three bears, jumped out of bed, ran all the way home, and never went back again. The three bears, of course, lived happily ever after.

The End

Chapter Nine

Work to Assign to Your Parents and Teachers

Well, why not? Your teachers give you assignments at school, and your parents give you chores to do at home. Now you can assign *them* a little "homework." Assign the rest of this to them – and your work is over!

To Parents and Teachers

You may want to go back and read this whole book. Then you'll know what your son, daughter, or student has learned about learning disabilities, and you'll have a chance to read it in plain language with easy-to-read definitions of some of the troublesome terms you may have found in some of your other readings. There's also a glossary at the end of the book where you'll find the definitions repeated in one handy section.

You'll find resources at the end of this chapter that may be especially useful. There are organizations you can write for more information, many of whom may have local chapters in your area. The national office of such organizations can let you know whom to contact. You'll also find two lists of books – one that's appropriate for you and another for books for children and adolescents with learning disabilities. One or two of these books are useful in helping brothers and sisters understand the problems their sibling is having, too.

If learning disabilities are new to you, then you may have dozens of questions and concerns that need attention. Sometimes nobody can answer those questions as well as someone who's already been through what you're going through right now. Other parents and teachers can be wonderful resources, and some of them are members of organizations listed in this book.

You may want to join one or more of these organizations. They can help you in many ways. If you're a parent, then support and information may be exactly what you're looking for right now. If you're a teacher, your membership in at least one of the organizations with a large parent membership will keep you in touch with the field in ways that professionals-only organizations cannot do.

But before you go back to the beginning of this book, or to the resources at the end, read the letters that follow. These are letters which tell you some of the things that youngsters with learning disabilities would like their parents and teachers to know. At the end of each letter, there's a space where your young person may have filled in some special concerns not covered in the letters. If not, you might give him or her a chance to use those spaces to reveal some of those concerns that there may not have been a chance to air before.

Dear Mom and Dad,

The most important thing I'd like for you to know is that I'm just a kid. The fact that I'm a kid – your kid – is more important than my learning disability or anything else about me.

Most of the time, the stuff I do – good and bad – is because I'm a kid, not because I have a learning disability. Being a kid is a full-time job, and it's a job that's supposed to be fun, at least part of the time. Don't focus so much on my learning disability that it becomes my full-time job.

Let me have some time just to mess around and be unstructured. I have to work so hard in school just to get by. I don't learn stuff in school just because I happen to hear it or to see it like so many kids do. I have to focus on it and really concentrate. It's exhausting!

I come home really tired and sometimes wrung out. Please give me some time to do what works best to relax me – maybe skateboarding or biking with a friend or alone; maybe just lying on my bed, or talking on the phone, or vegging out in front of the TV for a while. I need a break before I start the homework or tutoring. I'll be able to work more easily, faster, and more effectively if I don't have to start with the tired brain I come home with.

Please don't look at every messy paper or low grade as a sign that I'm a failure or you're a failure. Even straight-A students mess up sometimes.

And try to treat me like my brothers and sisters as much as possible. If everybody else gets to stay up a little late to watch a special on TV, don't say I have to go to bed on time otherwise I'll be impossible. Maybe I will be kind of difficult if I don't get enough sleep – but sometimes you don't notice that my brothers and sisters are, too.

If I'm on medication, help me take it just as the doctor orders. You might think it would be a good idea for me not to be on the medication on weekends, but if I get hyper when I'm at a slumber party or participating in sports, it'll cause problems for me socially. And my social skills are as important as my academic skills. Everybody needs friends, and I need all the help I can get. So talk to my doctor and explain everything to me before you decide to make changes in my medication.

Help me have friends. If I don't get many invitations to parties and sleepovers, plan activities for me that I can

*invite somebody to. Make them small at first, in case I
can't deal with too many people at once. Help me make
realistic choices – the kid who is mean to me at school
and who snubs me when he or she has a party might not
be a good choice. What about some other kid who needs a
friend, too?*

*If I'm old enough, let me help make decisions about
my program in school and outside of school. If my
brothers and sisters get to take soccer and karate and
ballet and gymnastics, and all I get is language therapy
or math tutoring, I may start feeling that my learning
disability and I are one and the same. Let me have some
activities that are fun and that I'm good at. I want to win
ribbons and trophies and be a member of a winning team,
too.*

*Be careful how you talk about me to the relatives.
If you only tell about my brother's successes in school
and all my sister's awards, and then how much my
tutoring or medication is costing, I'll feel like a failure
when I see my cousins at Grandma and Grandpa's.
Especially be careful what you say to that one aunt who
always enjoys telling everybody the worst things about
people.*

*I hate to say this, but don't be too easy on me, either. If
my brothers and sisters have to make up their beds, but I
don't because of the LD, I may seem to be glad, but really
I'll see it as just one more piece of evidence that I'm
incompetent. And they won't give me a break, either –
they'll resent me, and that can have long-term effects on
our relationship. So be sure I have duties, too – just don't
rate my ability to keep up without reminders, or expect
too much perfection!*

*I know how much you worry about me, and I'm really
scared I'll disappoint you. Sometimes when I refuse to
do things and am negative, it's because I'm afraid I can't
do it, and I'd almost rather have you think I'm a rotten*

kid who just won't *rather than a dumb kid who* can't. *Now and then give me a chance to talk about those fears. You can encourage me by saying, "I guess sometimes you'd rather not try than take a chance on not getting it right, huh?" and maybe "Don't worry – I'll help you, and I know that together we can get it right!"*

When I bring home work from school, even if it isn't very good, try to find something good to say first – "Wow! That's a really long paper! Your writing looks good on this page!" – before you notice the things the teacher wants me to do over. And when the teacher sends home a not-so-good paper and wants you to sign it and send it back, write something nice, too: "We will help work on this problem. I do like the way s/he is improving in punctuation." And sometimes, just sometimes, look at my work and only find good things to say.

Help me have a good place to do my schoolwork. Maybe I need to work at the kitchen table so that you can kind of supervise while you are fixing dinner or loading the dishwasher. Maybe I need a quieter spot, like a small desk in the corner of my room. I lose stuff, so try to keep a supply of pencils, paper, folders, and other school supplies somewhere. It would be best if you *keep them, because my stuff gets messy, and starting with dog-eared paper and chewed-up pencils just makes it harder for me to work.*

Also, help me find a place to keep everything I need to take to school. I'm not very well organized, and it's tough when I get to school and I've left something important at home. I probably need a backpack or school bag of some kind, and a place right by the door where I should be reminded to put it every night.

Please keep standing up for me when I need it. I know I get in trouble sometimes, and sometimes you need to get after me about it, but please don't get mad until you hear the whole story. Make sure I know that I'm not automatically in trouble every time the school calls. Keep an open mind – maybe, just maybe, this is the time they're calling because they want to tell you how much better I'm doing. Wouldn't you feel awful if you had said to me, "What have you done this time?" before you found out?

I guess the most important thing I have to tell you is that I love you, and I want you to be proud of me. Thanks for always being there, and loving me, too.

Love,

_____

P.S. Here are a few other things I want you to know:

_____

_____

_____

_____

_____

_____

_____

_____

Dear Teacher,

It's very important to me that you know me as a person, not "an LD." Please remember, even when you talk about me to other teachers, to call me by name or refer to me as "a student with LD" not "an LD" or "an ADD" or "a dyslexic." Keep reminding yourself and everyone else that I'm a person first, and that I'm much more than my learning disability.

I want you to know that I really do try hard. I have to try – I don't learn stuff just from being in the classroom and having it float around me like some kids do. I've never learned anything I wasn't really making myself pay attention to. And that's hard, and it's tiring. All kids stop paying attention once in a while. Sometimes I have to, just to give my brain and my eyes and my ears a rest. So I guess what I'm saying is that the worst thing you can ever say to me is, "You're just not trying!"

You need to understand, too, that sometimes when I won't do something you want me to do, it's because I'm afraid I can't. Sometimes I'd rather have you think I'm a rotten kid who won't than to know just how much I'm afraid I can't. If you want me to do something new, it helps a lot if you will say, "We're going to learn something new. I'll show you how to do it, and we'll work together, and then you'll be able to do it on your own!" You have no idea how much it helps me to hear you say, "I'm going to help you learn how to do this." Sometimes when you just say, "I know you can do this" it scares me unless you add "because I'm going to help you."

Please know that my parents are concerned about my work. They worry about it a lot. But they aren't my teachers, and sometimes if you expect them to be able to tutor me or teach me to do things I didn't finish in class, it's tough for them. When we get home at night, there's supper, and my brothers and sisters, and sports practices or music lessons, and baths, and everybody's homework to do. Some kids only have one parent at home, and some go to aftercare until six o'clock, so there's not all that much time, either.

If you're my regular teacher, notice how much time it takes me to do my work. If I'm really slow at copying my math problems before I do them, think about asking me to do just every other one. I will still have practiced some of every skill, and I will be able to finish in a reasonable time.

If you are having to make modifications for me in school, think about what modifications are reasonable. Doing every other math problem is sensible. An oral history test is, too. But an oral spelling test isn't because people only need to be able to spell words when they are writing. I may need to practice my spelling words orally if I'm an auditory learner, but I still need to be able to get them from my brain onto paper.

Help me keep my desk and maybe my locker organized. My parents may be able to help me keep my notebook in good order at home, but they aren't with me at school where my desk is. If you tell us to start on our social studies, and I take five minutes to dig out my books, it's a problem because I take longer to do the work than some of the others. Learning to be organized, which comes naturally to some students, is a real problem for us kids with LD.

If you're my resource or content mastery teacher, remember how important my regular class experience is to me. Help me find ways to work effectively in class, looking as much like the other kids as possible. If you can help me learn strategies to be organized and to work well, my self-concept will improve even more than if you worked just on my self-concept.

Let me know what my successes are. Remind me: "Remember when you said you'd never learn the times tables? You've learned them all the way up through the 8's! The 9's are going to be easy for you now!"

*Help me learn tricks for learning. Teach me mnemonic devices (like **G**eorge **E**liot's **O**ld **G**randfather **R**ode **A** **P**ig **H**ome **Y**esterday to help me spell Geography) or how to count or multiply on my fingers effectively. If I had a broken leg you'd let me use a crutch; teach me crutches for my broken arithmetic or memory. Once I've really overlearned the material, I'll throw away that crutch myself.*

Admire my abilities. Ask me about my gymnastics or trombone playing. Find out about the time I won the yoyo contest at the mall. Since you're the person who is mostly involved in focusing on my weaknesses, make it a point to remind me of my strengths, and to do that, you have to know what they are.

When I come into the room, start me out with something good – "I heard your other teacher bragging about your science project!" or even "Great jeans – are they new?" It doesn't have to be much – but if I came down the hall in a grumpy mood, I bet you can change it fast.

When you talk to my parents, you can probably help them a lot if you can start with something positive, too. How about, "Look at this increase in spelling! I'm really proud of this. Now let's see what we can do about getting this math homework in more consistently." They have been so used to hearing bad news that every time they get a call from school, they expect to hear that I'm in trouble again or failing something. They need to hear about my successes, too.

And remember, I'm their kid. They really want what's best for me. If they disagree with something you think I need to do, it's because they really think their way is best, or that your way just is not possible in our family situation. You may not know all the reasons – maybe you want one of them to read with me every night, and you don't know that one of them has to work nights or my big sister is babysitting all of us, and they'd rather not tell too much of our family business. Or maybe you want to send a homework list home every night to be signed, and you don't realize that I'm with my mom one week and my dad the next, and there are complications. If something is important, try to find another way. They really do love me, you know.

You are very important to me. I may not know why my program is set up the way it is, so help me understand it. Let me know that you are there to help, and that you see the kid inside who's trying very hard every day to be successful and as much like those regular kids as possible.

Please remember that I'm more than just my learning disability. I'm a kid who wants to be successful. I want to grow up to be somebody. You could be the teacher I'll always remember as the one who let me know I could succeed. Help me have a chance to reach my goals.

And, teacher, just in case I forget to say it sometimes – thanks.

Your student,

_____

P.S. Here are a few other things I want you to know:

_____

_____

_____

_____

_____

RESOURCES

Organizations

Learning Disabilities Association of America (formerly Association for Children and Adults with Learning Disabilities)
4156 Library Road
Pittsburgh PA 15234
(412) 341-1515

This group is for both parents and teachers as well as other people concerned about learning disabilities. They have local groups all over the country, so if parents write to the national address, they can get the address of the group nearest them. There are great newsletters, with news about TV shows about learning disabilities, movies, books, legislation, and meetings. Many state and local groups have their own newsletters, too, and some have "lending libraries" or books for sale, including many of the books I'm going to suggest later. Also, parents will find that nothing can take the place of the opportunity to meet with other parents who have gone through what you're going through. They can help you avoid pitfalls, and can help you find the sources of information you need, often much more quickly than we professionals can. If you can only join one organization, this is *the* one for parents.

Children and Adults with Attention Deficit Disorders
(CHADD)
499 N.W. 70th Avenue #308
Plantation, FL 33317
(305) 587-3700

The national organization provides a newsletter with information on a variety of issues concerning Attention Deficit Disorder. Information is available on local or regional chapters.

National Center for Learning Disabilities
381 Park Avenue South, Suite 1420
New York, NY 10016

This national organization has provided the first information
about learning disabilities that many people have received.
Through its public-service announcements on local and national
TV, it has reached many who felt they had nowhere to turn. Its
publications, including its annual publication *Their World,* and its
government briefings, including strong positions on current
educational trends, have been a powerful force in the field. The
Center also provides national referral to services and schools
through a computerized information system.

Orton Dyslexia Society
Chester Building, Suite 382
Baltimore, MD 21204-6020
(800) 222-3123

The Orton Dyslexia Society is comprised of parents and
professionals whose chief interest is dyslexia. While *dyslexia* is a
term that used to be reserved only for very severe reading
problems, it is now used by many people to include a variety of
types of learning disabilities. Still, the primary focus of the
society has been on reading problems. There may not be a local
group near you, but their publications and state and national
meetings provide a wealth of information.

Council for Exceptional Children (CEC) and its **Division for
Learning Disabilities** (DLD)
1920 Association Drive
Reston, VA 22091-1589

This umbrella organization, the Council for Exceptional
Children, is mainly a group for teachers and other professionals
concerned with children and adults with all kinds of special needs
(the gifted, as well as those with mental retardation, physical and
sensory handicaps, and those with learning disabilities). The

Division for Learning Disabilities is a special group for professionals interested in learning disabilities. CEC publishes two journals for its members, and DLD has two journals as well, one concerned with research on learning disabilities, and one that addresses a variety of issues.

Council for Learning Disabilities
P.O. Box 40303
Overland Park, KS 66204

The Council began as almost exclusively a professional organization, although there are now parents among its membership. It provides a newsletter, a journal, and state and national conferences.

There are also two information agencies that can provide sources on learning disabilities:

The National Information Center for Children and Youth with Learning Disabilities
P.O. Box 1492
Washington, DC 20012-1492
(800) 999-5599

The Center provides information on a variety of handicapping conditions, not just learning disabilities. Its focus includes children and adolescents, as well as those on the verge of adulthood.

HEATH Resource Center (Higher Education and the Handicapped)
1 Dupont Circle, Suite 789
Washington, DC 20036-1193
(800) 544-3284

HEATH is a national clearinghouse for information on college and other types of postsecondary education for individuals with all types of handicapping conditions. It offers many publications specifically dealing with college information for people with learning disabilities.

Books for Parents and Teachers

Bain, Lisa J. (1991). *A parent's guide to attention deficit disorders.* New York: Dell Publishing Co.

This book, which includes a foreword by C. Everett Koop, is a comprehensive guide for parents and teachers. A variety of treatment strategies are detailed, and a list of resource organizations is included.

Bloom, J. (1990). *Help me to help my child: A sourcebook for parents of learning disabled children.* Boston: Little, Brown.

A guidebook for parents, Bloom's book is organized by a set of questions parents may ask. It includes a 50-page section of appendices, including references and a glossary.

Copeland, E.D. & Love, V.L. (1990). *A teacher's handbook on attention disorders (ADHD & ADD).* Atlanta, GA: 3 C's of Childhood.

Parents as well as teachers will find this book useful. It details information on the neurological aspects of ADD and ADHD in a readable fashion, discusses the relationship between LD and ADD, and provides information on the roles of the child, teacher, parent, school, and physician in treating ADD.

Greenberg, G. S. & Horn, W.F. (1991). *Attention deficit hyperactivity disorder: Questions & answers for parents.* Champaign, IL: Research Press.

While Greenberg and Horn do discuss medication for ADHD, the primary focus of this book is on behavioral approaches to treatment, including timeout, charting, etc. This book is published by the primary source for materials on behavior modification approaches. Research Press.

Hayes, M.L. (1993). *You don't outgrow it: Living with learning disabilities.* Novato, CA: Academic Therapy Publications.

The problems of life as an adolescent or adult with learning disabilities has often been ignored in the literature. This common-sense guide is useful to the young adult and to parents and teachers as well. Resources and a glossary are included.

Ingersol, B. (1988). *Your hyperactive child: A parent's guide to coping with Attention Deficit Disorder.* New York: Doubleday.

This very readable book focuses specifically on Attention Deficit Disorder, a common problem among children with learning disabilities.

Lavin, P. (1989). *Parenting the overactive child: Alternatives to drug therapy.* Lanham, MD: Madison.

For parents who are definitely opposed to drug therapy for hyperactivity, Lavin provides behavioral alternatives, dietetic approaches, and a number of other techniques. Most controversial is Lavin's discussion of the appropriate use of punishment.

Lerner, J. (1992). *Learning disabilities: Theories, diagnosis, and teaching strategies* (6th ed.). Boston: Houghton Mifflin.

This is an outstanding, comprehensive text on learning disabilities for those who want thorough information and can handle college-text style.

Markoff, A.M. (1993). *Within reach: Academic achievement through parent-teacher communication.* Novato, CA: Academic Therapy Publications.

This guide for both parents and teachers provides a structure for making meetings about the child more productive and useful.

McCarney, S.B. & Bauer, A.M. (1991). *The parent's guide to learning disabilities: Helping your LD child succeed at home and school.* Columbia, MO: Hawthorne.

This guidebook is written in easy-to-use fashion, with an extensive table of contents showing specific learning or behavioral problems. The text lists a variety of possible solutions. A number of forms for homework charting, reward certificates, etc. are provided.

Osman, B.B., with Blinder, H. (1994). *No one to play with: The social side of learning disabilities.* (Rev. ed.) Novato, CA: Academic Therapy Publications.

This book focuses on the important issue of social skills in children with learning disabilities. Practical suggestions and guidance are given.

Silver, L.B. (1993). *Dr. Larry Silver's advice to parents on Attention-Deficit Hyperactivity Disorder.* Washington, DC: American Psychiatric Press.

This book answers common questions about ADHD, including clues parents may observe that suggest a need for referral to a professional. He also includes information on the current treatment and the types of professionals who can provide that treatment.

Silver, L.B. (1992). *The misunderstood child: A guide for parents of children with learning disabilities* (2nd ed.). Blue Ridge Summit, PA: TAB.

Silver is an MD who speaks authoritatively on learning disabilities and ADHD from the medical point of view. This book includes information on gifted children with LD and ADHD, a topic often overlooked.

Smith, S.L. (1991). *Succeeding against the odds: Strategies and insights from the learning disabled.* Los Angeles, CA: Jeremy P. Tarcher.

Smith gives useful information on success strategies developed by individuals with learning disabilities whose own struggles are detailed.

Books for Children and Adolescents with Learning Disabilities, ADD, and ADHD

Cummings, R. & Fisher, G. (1990). *The survival guide for teenagers with LD.* Indianapolis, IN: Free Spirit.

This book follows the authors' earlier book for elementary students with LD, and is aimed at students 13 and up. Transition issues are addressed as questions about the future, such as preparing for college and independent living.

Fisher, G. & Cummings, R. (1990). *The survival guide for kids with LD.* Indianapolis, IN: Free Spirit.

This book for mid-elementary age students through high school gives hints on school-related subjects as well as social assistance. Study techniques for specific school subjects, such as reading and math, are included.

Galvin, M. (1988). *Otto learns about his medicine: A story about medication for hyperactive children.* New York: Magination.

Most appropriate for children below 3rd or 4th grade, this books helps children understand hyperactive behavior and the role of medication in helping them control it through the adventures of Otto, a little car whose motor always goes too fast.

Gehret, J. (1991). *Eagle eyes: A child's guide to paying attention.* Fairport, NY: Verbal Images.

This beautiful book uses an imaginative story about a young boy and his sharp eyes to give information about Attention Deficit Disorders. The strong story and superb illustrations make it useful for many ages through elementary school. A brief resource section is included.

Gehret, J. (1990). *The don't-give-up kid and learning differences.* Fairport, NY: Verbal Images.

Alex, a boy with learning differences, wants to be an inventor like Thomas Edison when he grows up. His story, with beautiful illustrations, helps illustrate learning disabilities. A resource section promises more titles in the future.

Lasker, J. (1974). *He's my brother.* Chicago, IL: Albert Whitman.

For children below about third grade, this sensitive book tells the story of a brother with learning problems and ADHD without using the terms themselves. The book would be an excellent introduction for siblings of LD/ADD children.

Levine, M.D. (1993). *All kinds of minds.* Cambridge, MA: Educators Publishing Services.

Levine's book for 5th and 6th graders gives important information about LD through biographical sketches of youngsters with learning disabilities. Coping strategies and more information on each problem is then given so that young readers can apply information to their own problems.

Levine, M.D. (1990). *Keeping a head in school: A student's book about learning abilities and learning disorders.* Cambridge, MA: Educators Publishing Services.

A useful guide for students in high school, this book gives practical advice and assistance for making school survivable. There is plenty of focus on developing abilities rather than just remediating deficits.

Moss, D. (1989). *Shelly the hyperactive turtle.* Rockville, MD: Woodbine House.

This book, appropriate for young children with ADHD, helps explain the problems of hyperactivity and how medication can help.

Quinn, P.O. & Stern, J.M. (1991). *Putting on the brakes: Young people's guide to understanding Attention Deficit Hyperactivity Disorder (ADHD).* New York: Magination.

Designed for children from ages 8-13, this book provides good, basic information on AHDH. Included is information on causes, symptoms, and medication, as well as organizational suggestions to make homework and school learning easier. A short glossary is provided.

Shapiro, L.E. (1993). *Sometimes I drive my mom crazy, but I know she's crazy about me.* King of Prussia, PA: Childswork/Childsplay.

This story of a boy with ADHD includes information on the ways a variety of intervention strategies help him improve. The book includes information for teachers and parents, along with helpful charts for behavioral intervention.

Recorded Books for Print Handicapped and Blind

National Library Service for the Blind and Physically
    Handicapped
Library of Congress
1291 Taylor Street N.W.
Washington, DC 20542
(800) 424-8567

Recording for the Blind
20 Roszel Road
Princeton, NJ 08542
(609) 452-0606

Glossary

The following are some of the words used in this book, along with simple definitions and examples. Some of these words have other, general meanings that you might find in a regular dictionary, but I have included only the definitions for these words as I have used them in this book.

ADD: Attention Deficit Disorder. The name for a group of problems, such as hyperactivity, distractibility, etc. It is sometimes called ADHD (see below).

ADHD: Attention Deficit Hyperactivity Disorder. The name for a group of problems, such as hyperactivity, distractibility, etc. It is also sometimes called ADD (see above).

attention span: how long a person is able to pay attention to something. Many people with LD, ADD, or ADHD have short attention spans.

achievement tests: tests to see how much a student has learned in school subjects compared to other students. Individual achievement tests, the kind given to a single student by a diagnostician, often give scores as grade levels. In that case, a score of 4.2 in reading means that the student reads about as well as the average student in the second month of fourth grade. Group achievement tests, the kind given to large groups of students at one time, may give scores as percentiles. In that case, a score of 48 percentile in reading shown for a student in the fifth grade means that the student scored better than 48 fifth graders out of a hundred.

acronym: a word made up of the first letters of a title or other facts to make it easier to say or remember, such as HOMES for the Great Lakes (**H**uron,**O**ntario, **M**ichigan, **E**rie, **S**uperior)

auditory: having to do with hearing

auditory learner: a person who learns better with his or her ears, by hearing information. The person can use tapes, or his or her own voice, to help get information to the brain so it can be understood and remembered.

chronological age: actual age of a person in years and months

content mastery: a kind of special education in which a student may go to a special teacher for help on specific school assignments. Usually, this time is not scheduled, but the student may go after the regular teacher has taught a lesson, and it is time to go do the homework. The help can be on any assignment, from writing a report to doing a lab project on dissecting an earthworm!

depression: feeling sad and hopeless for a long period of time, even when there is no outside reason for it. Many people with LD, ADD, and ADHD have some depression and can ask a counselor for help in dealing with it.

diagnostician: a person trained to give tests and interpret them

distractibility: having the attention easily switched to something new, even when it is important to keep the attention on one thing. Many people with LD, ADD, or ADHD are very distractible in noisy settings or places where there is a lot of movement or activity.

dyslexia: a severe problem in learning, especially in reading, but sometimes in other areas of language also *dyslexic:* having the severe learning problem which is called *dyslexia*

EEG: stands for *electroencephalogram.* This is a medical test of brain activity. Sometimes problems in how a person's brain works can be found with this test. Many people with learning disabilities have normal EEG tests.

emotional disturbance: a problem in dealing with feelings and getting along with other people, which can affect school work and family life. Some students with emotional disturbance have so many problems that they behave in unusual ways and do not speak. Others may have many fears or other kinds of difficulties, including trouble with schoolwork. This is not the same as learning disability.

emotional problems: problems with feelings or getting along, either with school work or with other people. Some emotional problems are so severe that the student may need special help from a counselor. Students with learning disabilities may sometimes have emotional problems caused by their frustrations about their learning disabilities, but this is not the same as the problem called *emotional disturbance* (see the definition above), which is more severe.

flash cards: study cards, called *flash cards* because they are meant to be shown very quickly for a fast response. Now they are used even for more slow visual study. Usually, one side has a problem or question; the other has the problem or question repeated, along with the answer. Language flash cards have one language on one side, and the second language on the other.

highlighting: marking over words or sentences in a book with a transparent, light- or bright-colored marker so that the words will stand out. A technique for some visual learners.

hyper: a word used to describe a person who is much more active than the average person of the same age. It is short for *hyperactive.*

hyperactivity: far more activity than that shown by the average person of the same age

icon: a picture used on a computer screen to represent a name or instruction

impulsivity: doing or saying something without thinking first

intelligence test: a test made to measure how well a person thinks and solves problems. It is not supposed to measure actual learning, but ability to learn (see IQ test).

IQ: short for *intelligence quotient.* This is a score which tells the relationship between a person's actual age and the learning ability he or she showed on a particular test. People with learning disabilities often have above-average IQ scores.

IQ test: a kind of test used to measure a person's ability to learn. It is not supposed to show how much has already been learned, as an achievement test does, but how much the person might be able to learn in the right conditions.

jagged profile: a chart of different abilities for a particular student showing that he or she has some very high abilities and some very low ones. When the high scores and the low scores are connected by a line, it goes up and down sharply.

LD: the abbreviation for learning disability

learning disability: a problem in one or more areas of learning. It can be in a specific school subject, such as math, reading or language. It can be in a whole learning area, such as problems in learning things through seeing them or hearing them. While the cause may not be known, learning disability is *not* caused by mental retardation, poor eyesight, bad hearing, or emotional problems.

learning style: a way of learning. In this book, *learning style* means better learning ability when material is taken in either by seeing, for a visual learning style, or by hearing, for an auditory learning style. Other experts have different meanings for this term.

look-and-say approach: an approach to reading that begins with whole words, which the student memorizes and is then able to say as soon as he or she sees them. Later, new words are learned because they look similar to the old ones. Phonics skills are added only after many words are learned visually.

mental age: age in years and months of the average person whose thinking ability is similar to a particular person

mental retardation: a kind of severe learning problem in which almost all areas of a person's development are far slower than normal. This condition can include people who are still able to learn some school subjects and grow up to be self-supporting, as well as people who must have someone to care for them all of their lives. This is *not* the same thing as learning disability.

mnemonic device: a trick to help the memory, such as a sentence or poem to help remember a list of facts. Also called a *mnemonic.*

modification: change in the way something is done to make it possible for a student with a learning disability to show what he or she knows. For example, a student with a writing problem might be allowed to have an oral test, or have a scribe write his or her answers.

mood swings: sudden changes in the way a person feels, often without any real reason. A person with mood swings may be very happy one minute and sad or upset the next minute.

PL 94-142: The Education for All Handicapped Children Act. This law required schools to provide testing and special help for all students with handicaps, including learning disabilities, and to work with parents and children in deciding what kind of help was best.

perseveration: doing things over and over, even when it is not appropriate. Perseveration may include writing over the words on a worksheet several times, or pulling at a snag on clothing until it is ruined, or even continuing to talk on and on.

phonics: a term in reading, which refers to relating sounds to letters and groups of letters, and using them to figure out words

print impaired: a term to describe a person who has trouble reading printed material, because of a condition such as blindness or dyslexia

resource room: a classroom a student with learning disabilities may go to for less than half the day for help with specific school subjects

resource teacher: a teacher who works in a resource to help students with learning disabilities. Sometimes the term means a teacher who is available to help other teachers, too.

Ritalin: a medication often used to help people with hyperactivity or other ADD behaviors *rough draft:* the first copy of a paper that a student writes. It is not supposed to be the one that will be turned in, so the student will expect to make changes and corrections to improve it before recopying it.

scribe: a person who writes the answers for a student with a learning disability. The scribe is not allowed to change anything, but only to write exactly what the student says to write.

short attention span: ability to pay attention for only a very short period of time

sight distractibility: being unable to pay attention to just one thing when there are things to see in the surrounding area

sound distractibility: being able to pay attention to just one thing when there are other sounds in the surrounding area

spell checker: a special program on a computer that allows the user to check the spelling of all of the words he or she has used in a piece of writing. The spell checker can only check spelling errors, not errors in usage (there-their).

20/20 vision: ability to see normally for distance. A person with 20/20 vision can see, without glasses, at 20 feet what a normal person can see at 20 feet. A person with 20/40 vision can see at 20 feet what a normal person can see at 40 feet, and so forth. This does not tell how well the person understands what he or she sees.

visual: having to do with sight

visual learner: a person who learns better with his or her eyes, by seeing information. The person can use pictures or written words, real or in the mind's eye, to help get information to the brain so it can be understood and remembered.

word processing: a computer program that allows the user to write information as he or she would on a typewriter, but the user can store it, move it around, and add to it or delete from it before having it printed by the computer